PREFACE

1. Scope

This publication provides joint doctrine for the planning, command and control, and employment of resources within the Defense Transportation System.

2. Purpose

This publication has been prepared under the direction of the Chairman of the Joint Chiefs of Staff (CJCS). It sets forth joint doctrine to govern the activities and performance of the Armed Forces of the United States in joint operations and provides the doctrinal basis for US military coordination with other US Government departments and agencies during operations and for US military involvement in multinational operations. It provides military guidance for the exercise of authority by combatant commanders and other joint force commanders (JFCs) and prescribes joint doctrine for operations, education, and training. It provides military guidance for use by the Armed Forces in preparing their appropriate plans. It is not the intent of this publication to restrict the authority of the JFC from organizing the force and executing the mission in a manner the JFC deems most appropriate to ensure unity of effort in the accomplishment of the overall objective.

3. Application

a. Joint doctrine established in this publication applies to the Joint Staff, commanders of combatant commands, subunified commands, joint task forces, subordinate components of these commands, and the Services.

b. The guidance in this publication is authoritative; as such, this doctrine will be followed except when, in the judgment of the commander, exceptional circumstances dictate otherwise. If conflicts arise between the contents of this publication and the contents of Service publications, this publication will take precedence unless the CJCS, normally in coordination with the other members of the Joint Chiefs of Staff, has provided more current and specific guidance. Commanders of forces operating as part of a multinational (alliance or coalition) military command should follow multinational doctrine and procedures ratified by the United States. For doctrine and procedures not ratified by the United States, commanders should evaluate and follow the multinational command's doctrine and procedures, where applicable and consistent with US law, regulations, and doctrine.

For the Chairman of the Joint Chiefs of Staff:

CURTIS M. SCAPARROTTI
Lieutenant General, U.S. Army
Director, Joint Staff

Intentionally Blank

- Adds language on United States Transportation Command's (USTRANSCOM's) role as the Department of Defense (DOD) Distribution Process Owner.

- Introduces the Integrated Data Environment/Global Transportation Network Convergence as the designated DOD system for in-transit visibility.

- Reflects the correct name of USTRANSCOM's Army Service Component Command, the Military Surface Deployment and Distribution Command, and its new status as a major subordinate command of the US Army Materiel Command.

- Refines USTRANSCOM's roles and responsibilities for DOD Military Customs and Border Clearance Program (CBCP).

- Adds language on the Department of Homeland Security and its relationship to DOD.

- Expands descriptions of sealift transportation resource.

- Adds a section under land resources on continental US commercial resources.

- Adds a section under land resources on Defense Transportation Coordination Initiative.

- Expands a section under land resources on outside the continental US common-user land transportation.

- Expands the geographic combatant commander's responsibilities in the theater resources section.

- Expands the description of each of the Service's assets in the pre-positioning and forward stocking section.

- Adds a section addressing automated identification technology.

- Defines USTRANSCOM's responsibilities for DOD Military CBCP.

Intentionally Blank

TABLE OF CONTENTS

EXECUTIVE SUMMARY
COMMANDER'S OVERVIEW

- **Gives an overview of the Defense Transportation System**

- **Identifies the Responsibilities, Roles, and Interrelationships of the Principal Agencies involved in the Defense Transportation System**

- **Describes Types of Transportation Resources**

- **Explains Employment of the Defense Transportation System**

The Defense Transportation System

The Defense Transportation System is multifaceted, resulting in a versatility that supports the joint force across the range of military operations.

The Defense Transportation System (DTS) is that portion of the worldwide transportation infrastructure that supports Department of Defense (DOD) transportation needs in peace and war. It consists of two major elements: military (organic) and commercial (nonorganic) resources. These resources include aircraft, ships, barges, rail and road assets, pipelines, services, and systems organic to, contracted for, or controlled by DOD. DTS infrastructure, including seaports, aerial ports, railways, highways, pipeline pumping and terminal stations, automated information systems, as well as supporting services, such as in-transit visibility (ITV), customs, and traffic management, are vital elements of the DOD capability to project power worldwide.

Global Transportation Management

Global transportation management (GTM) refers to an integrated process that includes coordinated efforts in the planning, programming, budgeting, and execution process, development of unified or coordinated management procedures and systems for deliberate and crisis action planning, and application of DOD and civil transportation systems through exercises, operations, and centralized traffic management.

In-Transit Visibility

To promote an effective GTM and ITV, the supporting transportation and distribution cyberspace capabilities must be effective, efficient, and secure. ITV is the capability to employ information technology resources to track the identity, status, and location of DOD units, non-unit cargo (excluding bulk petroleum, oils, and lubricants), passengers, patients, and personal property from origin to consignee or destination across the range of military operations.

Interrelationships

Secretary of Defense

The Secretary of Defense (SecDef) is responsible for transportation planning and operations within DOD.

Chairman of the Joint Chiefs of Staff

The Chairman of the Joint Chiefs of Staff (CJCS). CJCS reviews and evaluates movement requirements and resources, apportions capability, and allocates capability when required.

United States Transportation Command (USTRANSCOM)

The Commander, United States Transportation Command (CDRUSTRANSCOM):

- Provides transportation and common-user port management and terminal services for DOD as well as non-DOD agencies upon request.
- Exercises combatant command (command authority) (COCOM) of all assigned forces as authorized by the "Forces for Unified Commands" Memorandum as incorporated in the Global Force Management Implementation Guidance.
- Exercises responsibility for global air, land, and sea transportation planning (deliberate and crisis action).

USTRANSCOM Transportation Component Commands achieve optimum intermodal capability through integration of common-user transportation systems and resources.

Air Mobility Command (AMC) is a major command of the US Air Force. As a transportation component of United States Transportation Command (USTRANSCOM), AMC provides common-user air mobility and aeromedical evacuation transportation services to deploy, employ, sustain, and redeploy US forces on a global basis.

Military Sealift Command (MSC) is a major command of the US Navy. As a transportation component of USTRANSCOM, MSC provides common-user and exclusive use sealift transportation services to deploy, employ, sustain, and redeploy US forces on a global basis.

Military Surface Deployment and Distribution Command (SDDC) is an operational level Army force designated by the Secretary of the Army as the Army Service Component Command of USTRANSCOM and a major subordinate command of US Army Materiel Command. As a transportation component of USTRANSCOM, SDDC provides worldwide common-use ocean terminal services and traffic management services to deploy, employ, sustain, and redeploy US forces on a global basis.

Geographic Combatant Commanders

Geographic combatant commanders (GCCs), in coordination with CDRUSTRANSCOM and other supporting commanders, are jointly responsible for the deployment of forces from origin to destination. Supported and supporting commanders' planners integrate component requirements and develop the time-phased force and deployment data (TPFDD), which identifies force requirements to support a particular plan and provides routing data from origin to destination.

Military Departments

The Military Departments retain the responsibility for organizing, training, equipping, and providing the logistic support (including Service-organic transportation) of their respective forces.

Department of Transportation

Under national defense emergency conditions, the Secretary of Transportation (SECTRANS) will govern the priority use of all civil transportation and the allocation of its capacity to meet essential civil and military needs. Federal transportation agencies will carry out their plans in compliance with SECTRANS policy.

Commercial Transportation Service Providers

The commercial transportation community has significant capacity to augment DOD and other federal resources. For example, programs such as Civil Reserve Air Fleet (CRAF) and Voluntary Intermodal Sealift Agreement make up a significant portion of US wartime lift capability.

Transportation Resources

Air Mobility

AMC is responsible for all commercial air tenders and the worldwide express international commercial express package service contract. AMC C-5, C-17, C-130, KC-10, and KC-135 aircraft are stationed in continental United States (CONUS) and operate through a combination of active, Air Force Reserve, and Air National Guard resources (when mobilized) to provide common-user air mobility under the COCOM of

CDRUSTRANSCOM. GCCs exercise COCOM over assigned air mobility forces and either operational control (OPCON) or tactical control over attached air mobility forces. Service organic air mobility forces are those assets that are an integral part of a specific Service, component, or major command and primarily support the requirements of the organization to which they are assigned. CRAF is designed to augment DOD capability with contractually committed US civil aircraft, aircrews, and support structure when requirements exceed DOD air mobility capability and voluntary support is either insufficient or unavailable. Airlift capacity is also available from foreign allies and North Atlantic Treaty Organization entities via cooperative military airlift agreements, acquisition and cross-servicing agreements (ACSAs), and similar arrangements.

Sealift

Shipping resources can be classified into three pools: United States Government (USG)-owned, US flag commercial, and foreign flag commercial assets.

When an expansion of US Government requirements occurs such that organic and voluntary US and foreign flag shipping can no longer provide sufficient lift capacity, Department of Defense may elect to activate prenegotiated agreements with US flag vessels.

USG-Owned Assets. DOD (MSC) maintains a fleet of operating organic vessels as well as a fleet in a reduced operating status (ROS). Department of Transportation (Maritime Administration) maintains a fleet of vessels in a ROS that can be turned over to MSC to operate during a contingency.

US Flag Fleet. Ships operating under a US flag are routinely chartered by MSC to meet both long-term and unique government shipping demands.

Foreign Flag Ships. When US flag ships are unavailable, foreign flag ships can be acquired for DOD use through three different methods: voluntary charter, allied shipping agreements, and requisitioning of effective US control shipping.

Land

Military SDDC maintains transportation agreements and all commercial carrier costing information necessary to move shipments within the US via surface transportation. This includes approving commercial carriers to conduct business with the DOD; evaluating carrier performance; and maintaining carrier tender information. SDDC owns and manages the Defense Freight Railway Interchange Fleet. (DFRIF). The DFRIF is composed of all cars purchased by, or in-leased on behalf of any branch of the armed forces for loaded movement by commercial railroads throughout North America. The commercial transportation industry has substantial capability available to meet the CONUS transportation needs of DOD. SDDC administers the Contingency Response Program which supports the acquisition of domestic civil transportation resources during military deployments. The Defense Transportation Coordination Initiative is a joint USTRANSCOM, Defense Logistics Agency (DLA), and Services program which, under SDDC oversight, uses a commercial third-party logistics provider to manage freight movements in CONUS. Outside the continental United States (OCONUS), assigning responsibility for common-user land transportation (CULT) is a function of the GCC's directive authority for logistics, and it is up to each GCC to outline this in the operation plan and supporting plans. Under CULT, land transportation assets are normally under the OPCON of the Army component commander, who coordinates all planning and requirements for the use of DOD-controlled land transportation equipment and facilities designated common-use in theater.

Theater

There are numerous transportation and mobility resources available to GCCs. The only source of organic resources to US forces in overseas areas consists of air and surface units assigned to the GCC for common-user transportation service. Theater-assigned common-user transportation assets are under the COCOM of the respective GCC. A frequently used means of augmenting or expanding the GCC's transportation capability is host-nation support (HNS). HNS, negotiated through bilateral or multilateral agreements, provides for a nation to either accept responsibility for a particular function within its borders (e.g., aerial port of debarkation [APOD] cargo clearance) or designate civilian and/or military resources to be used in that capacity under military control. Negotiated on a bilateral basis usually with multinational partners and sometimes with other eligible countries, ACSAs allow for the exchange of logistic support, supplies, and services during combined exercises, training deployments, operations, and for unforeseen circumstances and contingencies.

Port Operations

Military and commercial ports are critical components of DTS supporting the air and maritime movement of unit- and non-unit personnel, equipment, and cargo. These ports could be owned and operated by SDDC, AMC, a Service, GCC, or commercial or host nation authorities. They may be either sophisticated fixed locations or heavily dependent on deployable mission support forces or joint logistics over-the-shore (JLOTS) assets to accomplish the mission. The single port manager performs those functions necessary to support the strategic flow of deploying and redeploying forces, unit equipment, and sustainment supply in the seaports of embarkation and aerial ports of embarkation and hand-off to the GCC in the seaports of debarkation and APODs.

Pre-Positioning and Forward Stocking

DOD pre-positioned force, equipment, or supplies programs are both land- and sea-based. They are critical programs for reducing closure times of combat and support forces needed in the early stages of a contingency. The US Army and US Marine Corps pre-positioning programs consist of combat and combat support or sustainment capabilities, to include in-stream discharge and JLOTS capabilities. DLA's OCONUS distribution depots offer opportunities to forward position stock of OCONUS customers and enhance the theater distribution system by forward stocking high usage items closer to the operational area, thereby enabling parts and supplies to be distributed in a timely manner.

Intermodal Systems

Intermodal refers to the transferring of passengers or transshipping of cargo among two or more modes of transportation. In concert with intermodal distribution, containerization facilitates and optimizes carrying of cargo via multiple modes of transport (highway, rail, sea, inland waterway, and air) without intermediate handling of the contents. Intermodalism and the use of the DOD intermodal container system are integral to the efficiency and effectiveness of DTS support to joint operations.

Employment of the Defense Transportation System

Requirements Determination and Submission

Movement requirements are established by competent authority within the Joint Staff, the Military Departments, combatant commands, other DOD and USG departments and agencies, and the Executive Branch of the government. The Deployment and Distribution

Operations Center Fusion Center is the command and control (C2) structure used by USTRANSCOM to exercise C2 of DTS and is grounded in the principle of centralized control of DTS and the decentralized execution of qualified movement requirements. For wartime and contingency movement requirements, the supported combatant commander (CCDR), in coordination with supporting commanders and Services, establishes movement requirements. This is accomplished by developing a deployment and/or redeployment TPFDD in Joint Operation Planning and Execution System (JOPES). The supporting and supported commanders, and their components, review this TPFDD, source the various requirements, and then refine or establish a detailed transportation timeline. When completed, USTRANSCOM and supported CCDRs validate requirements in JOPES for the appropriate transportation component command (TCC) to plan, schedule, and execute movement.

Planning and Allocation of Resources - Wartime or Contingency

The supported CCDR develops a concept of operations based upon guidance in Chairman of the Joint Chiefs of Staff instruction (CJCSI) 3110.01, *Joint Strategic Capabilities Plan*, and *Guidance for Employment of the Force*. Subordinate component commanders are then tasked to determine specific forces (unit) and supply (non-unit) requirements (including personnel replacements) and the recommended time phasing of these requirements. The component commands' force and support requirements are submitted to the supported CCDR, who integrates them with any other requirements to develop the TPFDD. The strategic movement of these requirements is then analyzed against the specified transportation assets found in CJCSI 3110.11, *Mobility Supplement to Joint Strategic Capabilities Plan*, using the Joint Flow and Analysis System for Transportation in order to determine gross transportation feasibility of the plan.

Execution - Contingency and Wartime

Upon receipt of a warning order, alert order, or other indication of a potential deployment, USTRANSCOM establishes communications with the logistics directorate of a joint staff, the supported and supporting CCDRs, the Services, and TCCs. USTRANSCOM also reviews force deployment and sustainment plans; develops feasibility estimates; monitors port, transportation, and lines of communications; develops strategic airlift and sealift schedules. USTRANSCOM coordinates the execution of CJCS and CCDR lift allocation decisions for transportation resources that support the plans being executed.

In-Transit Visibility Reporting

The Integrated Data Environment/Global Transportation Network Convergence (IGC) is a single system that integrates information from a variety of DTS automated information systems to provide ITV and C2 data support. IGC enables a common logistics picture, distribution visibility, and material asset/ITV. Global Air Transportation Execution System is the primary port of embarkation and port of debarkation systems for sealift and air mobility, respectively. Cargo Movement Operations System is the primary system at US Air Force non-AMC-owned organizations. AMC schedules and manages the execution of organic and AMC chartered strategic airlift through the Global Decision Support System.

Employment of Military Movement Resources During a Disruption of Civil Transportation in the Continental United States

If CONUS civil transportation service is disrupted and SecDef so directs, the military-owned capability specified in this section can be applied within CONUS to help meet military movement requirements. The Services, CCDRs, DLA, SDDC, and AMC are responsible for providing data or making available vehicles and aircraft with associated operations, maintenance, and administration.

CONCLUSION

This publication provides joint doctrine for the planning, command and control, and employment of resources within the DTS.

CHAPTER I
THE DEFENSE TRANSPORTATION SYSTEM

> *"Victory is the beautiful, bright-colored flower. Transport is the stem without which it could never have blossomed."*
>
> **Winston Churchill,** ***The River War,*** **1899**

1. Purpose

This chapter provides a general overview of the Defense Transportation System (DTS) and its role in supporting US national security objectives worldwide. **DTS is multifaceted, resulting in a versatility that supports the joint force across the range of military operations.**

2. Overview

a. **Background.** DTS is that portion of the worldwide transportation infrastructure that supports Department of Defense (DOD) transportation needs in peace and war. It consists of two major elements: military (organic) and commercial (nonorganic) resources. These resources include aircraft, ships, barges, rail and road assets, pipelines, services, and systems organic to, contracted for, or controlled by DOD. DTS infrastructure, including seaports, aerial ports, railways, highways, pipeline pumping and terminal stations, automated information systems, as well as supporting services, such as in-transit visibility (ITV), customs, and traffic management, are vital elements of the DOD capability to project power worldwide. Combining the capabilities of transportation assets into an integrated network optimizes the use of airlift, sealift, and land transportation resources, provides greater visibility over operations, and expedites the transition from peace to war. Transportation procedures and organizational responsibilities as they relate to peacetime and wartime requirements should remain unchanged regardless of the type of operation being conducted. The increased intensity necessary to support operations should not require a new set of procedures and systems. Transportation processes and procedures are performed in accordance with the *Defense Transportation Regulation (DTR) 4500.9-R.* This standardization allows transportation forces to train during times of peace in the same manner in which they would operate during war or a contingency and provides the inherent flexibility to effectively and quickly support any type of military operation. In this regard, the aggregate transportation capability exercised through DTS is a critical enabling instrument that allows DOD to support the objectives and strategies of the President and Secretary of Defense (SecDef). The Commander, United States Transportation Command (CDRUSTRANSCOM), develops and directs the Joint Deployment and Distribution Enterprise to globally project strategic national security capabilities; accurately sense the operating environment; provide end-to-end distribution process visibility and identify potential opportunities for performance improvement; and provide responsive support of joint, United States Government (USG), and SecDef-approved multinational and nongovernmental logistical requirements. In this capacity, except for those assets that are Service-organic or theater-assigned, CDRUSTRANSCOM exercises combatant command (command authority) (COCOM) of the

The Defense Transportation System serves a vital role in supporting US national security worldwide.

assigned transportation assets and is the DOD single manager for transportation. CDRUSTRANSCOM aligns traffic management and transportation single manager responsibilities to achieve optimum responsiveness, effectiveness, and economy. CDRUSTRANSCOM establishes and maintains relationships between DOD and the commercial transportation industry. The principles and considerations discussed in Joint Publication (JP) 4-0, *Joint Logistics,* provide useful guidance to this end. This publication describes those core logistic capabilities that are essential to success, and offers a framework within which joint logistics can be planned, executed, and controlled effectively.

b. **Support of National Strategy.** As shown in Figure I-1, DTS consists of US military, commercial, and host nation (HN) assets. A modern, flexible, and responsive transportation network capable of integrating military, commercial, and HN resources must exist in order to project US military power anywhere in the world. United States Transportation Command (USTRANSCOM), in coordination with the geographic combatant commanders (GCCs), is the focal point for the integration of DOD transportation procedures and systems to ensure strategic mobility capabilities are maintained, to include global air, land, and sea transportation to meet national security needs.

c. **Global Transportation Management (GTM).** GTM refers to an integrated process that includes coordinated efforts in the planning, programming, budgeting, and execution process, development of unified or coordinated management procedures and systems for deliberate and crisis action planning, and application of DOD and civil transportation systems through exercises, operations, and centralized traffic management. DOD movement requirements are numerous, ranging from normal peacetime operations to major combat

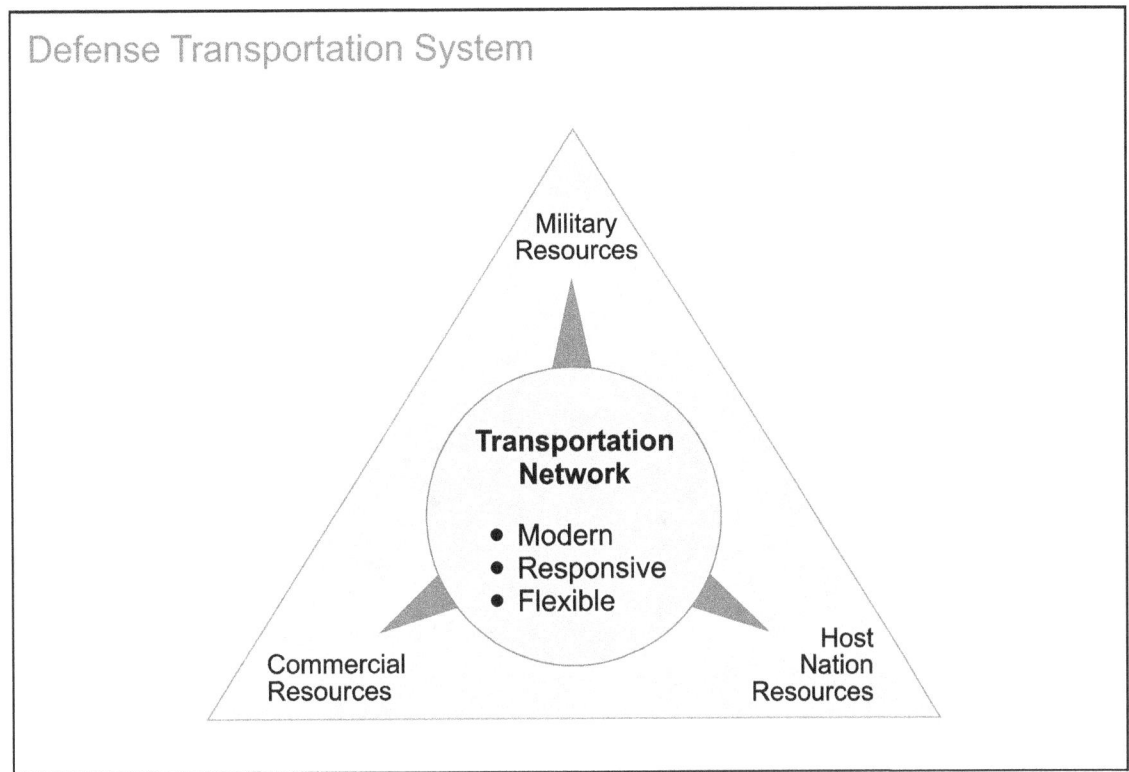

Figure I-1. Defense Transportation System

operations in which the Nation's transportation system will be severely taxed, and the transition period from peacetime to war may be extremely short. These movements take place across the global distribution network, a complex array of capabilities and providers, operating across multiple theaters, under the direction of numerous commands and agencies. The GTM process establishes an integrated transportation system, providing the most effective use of air, sea, and land transportation resources from origin to destination. The object of GTM is to achieve responsive transportation capability for all phases of military operations.

(1) SecDef has designated CDRUSTRANSCOM as the DOD distribution process owner (DPO). The DPO's role is to coordinate, synchronize, and oversee the DOD distribution system to provide interoperability, synchronization, and alignment of DOD-wide end-to-end distribution.

(2) This responsibility was expanded in the Unified Command Plan (UCP) 2011, which designated CDRUSTRANSCOM as responsible for the synchronized planning of global distribution operations in coordination with other combatant commands (CCMDs), the Services, and as directed, appropriate USG departments and agencies. In this additional role, CDRUSTRANSCOM leads a collaborative operation and campaign planning effort that includes combatant commanders (CCDRs), Services, combat support agencies, DOD agencies, and as appropriate, interagency, commercial partners, and allied/friendly/cooperating nations. Within DOD's phase 0 operation and campaign planning construct, the efforts of the synchronized planning forum focus on shaping the future of distribution. Key CDRUSTRANSCOM objectives include:

Global transportation management ensures that transitions between peace and wartime activities are smooth and rapid.

(a) Synchronizing efforts between global and theater distribution plans (TDPs).

(b) Identifying potential gaps, threats, and vulnerabilities to distribution operations, along with opportunities to mitigate these risks.

(c) Producing a comprehensive, integrated understanding of distribution that informs posture planning.

(d) Leveraging security cooperation opportunities to sustain and enhance the global distribution network.

(e) Building relationships, improving distribution infrastructure, and enhancing "access" as required to enable distribution operations.

(f) Enhancing distribution capabilities.

d. **In-Transit Visibility (ITV).** To promote an effective GTM and ITV, the supporting transportation and distribution cyberspace capabilities must be effective, efficient, and secure. ITV is the capability to employ information technology resources to track the identity, status, and location of DOD units, nonunit cargo (excluding bulk petroleum, oils, and lubricants [POL]), passengers, patients, and personal property from origin to consignee or destination across the range of military operations. The Integrated Data Environment/Global Transportation Network Convergence (IGC) is the designated DOD system for ITV.

See Chapter IV, "Employment of the Defense Transportation System," for a more detailed discussion of ITV and IGC.

e. **Transportation Requirements.** Commanders and planners at the strategic, operational, and tactical levels require a detailed supporting database to provide adequate force, deployment, employment, sustainment, and retrograde information. The database prepared through the Joint Operation Planning and Execution System (JOPES) provides information to the supported and supporting CCDRs, USTRANSCOM, subordinate joint force commanders (JFCs), the Services, and DOD agencies to assist in identifying time-phased deployment requirements. Planners use specialized applications programs in JOPES and interface with other application programs through JOPES, to create a time-phased force and deployment data (TPFDD) computer file. Use of the automated database is essential to the timely exchange of detailed force and other deployment data. CCDRs, subordinate JFCs, components, and supporting commands must enter accurate transportation requirements into JOPES as soon as they are known. USTRANSCOM and its components use this data to gain a close approximation of the transportation assets that may be needed to move the requirements. Chairman of the Joint Chiefs of Staff Manual (CJCSM) 3122.02, *Joint Operation Planning and Execution System Volume III Crisis Action Time-Phased Force and Deployment Data Development and Deployment Execution,* is the primary source document for use of the automated database to direct a crisis response.

f. **General Considerations.** Although the level of detail may vary depending on the scope of the mission and the echelon of command where a transportation requirement is being worked, there are several general considerations that influence transportation planning and capability. They include those provided in Figure I-2.

g. **Critical Infrastructure Protection.** Central to all plans that use DTS is the assurance that physical infrastructures (such as ports and road and rail systems), command and control (C2) systems, and intelligence infrastructures will be available when needed. As the threat of asymmetrical attacks on those infrastructures grows, it is imperative that organizations which rely on DTS identify critical infrastructures that, if compromised, could jeopardize mission accomplishment of the supported CCDR. Organizations must take actions to mitigate vulnerabilities and ensure that those critical assets will be available to meet mission requirements.

Transportation Planning and Capability Considerations

- Amount and availability of forces and materiel to be moved

- Availability and characteristics of movement resources, both military and civilian

- Priorities established for the movement

- Duration and time available for planning the movement

- Reception and throughput capabilities (including host-nation support) of ports of embarkation and ports of debarkation

- Strategic transportation sustainment capability

- The threat and potential attrition

- Requirements to convoy

- Degree of protection provided to the lines of communications

- Total asset visibility, including in-transit visibility and accessibility of items in the pipeline

- Mode selection based upon the most economical transportation resource to accomplish the movement within acceptable time limits

- Availability of materials handling equipment and container handling equipment

Figure I-2. Transportation Planning and Capability Considerations

CHAPTER II
INTERRELATIONSHIPS

"If you don't have my army supplied, and keep it supplied, we'll eat your mules."

William Tecumseh Sherman's warning to an army quartermaster before the departure of Sherman's army from Chattanooga toward Atlanta, 1864.

1. Purpose

This chapter identifies the responsibilities, roles, and interrelationships of the principal agencies involved in DTS.

2. Background

Situations with a potential to create civil transportation emergencies range from local labor strikes and natural disasters to war. Since a large portion of the emergency transportation capability needed by DOD is in civil sector resources, **close coordination among a wide variety of military and USG departments and agencies will be required to meet contingency transportation requirements.**

3. Department of Defense

a. **SecDef is responsible for transportation planning and operations within DOD.** SecDef designated the Deputy Under SecDef (Logistics and Materiel Readiness) to establish policies and provide guidance to DOD components concerning the efficient and effective use of DTS. SecDef designated CDRUSTRANSCOM as DOD single manager for transportation (other than for Service-organic or theater-assigned transportation assets) during times of peace and war. SecDef designated the DOD Chief Information Officer (CIO) to establish policy and guidance concerning interoperability and information assurance requirements needed for effective, efficient, and secure DTS operations in cyberspace.

b. **The Chairman of the Joint Chiefs of Staff (CJCS). CJCS reviews and evaluates movement requirements and resources, apportions capability, and allocates capability when required. The CJCS:**

(1) Establishes procedures, in coordination with the Assistant Deputy Under Secretary of Defense (Transportation Policy), the Secretaries of the Military Departments, and the Defense Logistics Agency (DLA), for the submission of movement requirements by DOD user components to USTRANSCOM and for the submission of evaluated requirements and capabilities by USTRANSCOM and the transportation component commands (TCCs) to CJCS.

(2) Prescribes a movement priority system in agreement with Uniform Materiel Movement and Issue Priority System (UMMIPS) that will ensure responsiveness to meet the requirements of the using forces.

(3) Monitors the capabilities of USTRANSCOM common-user transportation resources to provide airlift, sealift, continental United States (CONUS) land transportation, common-user ocean terminal service, and aerial port service based upon the requirements of DOD components.

(4) Assigns movement priorities in support of DOD.

(5) Apportions intertheater air mobility assets through the Chairman of the Joint Chiefs of Staff Instruction (CJCSI) 3110.11, *Mobility Supplement to the Joint Strategic Capabilities Plan.*

(6) Adjudicates competing lift requirements as requested by USTRANSCOM or the CJCS Joint Transportation Board (JTB).

Appendix B, "Charter of the Chairman of the Joint Chiefs of Staff Joint Transportation Board," outlines the functions, responsibilities, and membership of the CJCS JTB.

(7) Acts on the recommendations of the CJCS JTB with respect to the establishment of priorities and allocations for the use of air mobility, sealift, and surface transportation capability.

c. **The CDRUSTRANSCOM:**

(1) Provides transportation and common-user port management and terminal services for DOD as well as non-DOD agencies upon request.

(2) Exercises COCOM of all assigned forces as authorized by the "Forces for Unified Commands" Memorandum as incorporated in the Global Force Management Implementation Guidance. (Reserve Component forces only when mobilized or ordered to active duty for other than training.)

(3) Exercises responsibility for global air, land, and sea transportation planning (deliberate and crisis action).

(4) Acts as DOD focal point for items moving through the transportation system.

(5) Exercises responsibility for intertheater (non-theater assigned) aeromedical evacuation.

(6) Oversees the responsibilities listed below:

(a) Providing supported CCDRs with the coordinated transportation planning expertise required during the deliberate and crisis action planning processes participating in all seven steps of the joint operation planning process with the supported CCMD. This includes reviewing the Joint Strategic Capabilities Plan (JSCP) tasking, Guidance for Employment of the Force (GEF), analyzing supported CCDR requirements registered in JOPES (force and non-unit cargo and/or personnel) for transportation feasibility, and advising the supported CCDR of changes required to produce a force and sustainable deployment concept. Upon approval of the supported CCDR's plan, provide plan maintenance support as required.

(b) Providing deployment estimates and total lift asset availability to the President, SecDef, and supported CCDRs for development of alternative courses of action (COAs) and optimal flow of forces during crisis action planning. CDRUSTRANSCOM advises the supported CCDRs and CJCS concerning use of, or changes to, lift capabilities.

(c) Assisting the supported CCDRs during deployment and ensuring validated movement requirements are routed and scheduled. During sustainment, redeployment, and reconstitution, CDRUSTRANSCOM considers efficient use of intertheater lift resources. CDRUSTRANSCOM assists CJCS by recommending reallocation of intertheater assets to optimize their use and support plan execution during deployment, employment, reconstitution, redeployment, and sustainment. CDRUSTRANSCOM refers problems with recommended COAs to the CJCS JTB for resolution or adjudication if a balance of transportation requirements and capabilities cannot be maintained.

(d) Interfacing, as executive agent for DOD Customs, with US Customs and Border Protection (CBP), state customs, and agriculture officials, CPB provides agriculture inspections of DOD personnel, materiel, and equipment returning to the customs territory of the US.

(e) Developing and maintaining integrated, effective, efficient, and secure ITV, transportation, and distribution cyberspace capabilities for DOD. IGC provides that capability and is the designated ITV system for DOD. IGC also provides C2 functionality for USTRANSCOM and is integrated into the Global Command and Control System (GCCS) and the Global Combat Support System. USTRANSCOM provides other capabilities to support end-to-end deployment and distribution planning and execution. For additional information, refer to Chapter IV, "Employment of the Defense Transportation System." GCCS is a national C2 system.

For additional information on GCCS, refer to JP 6-0, Joint Communications System.

(f) Developing policies and procedural guidance through the CCDRs, in collaboration with the DOD components, USG border clearance activities, and foreign governments, to ensure efficiency and uniformity in the implementation of the DOD Military Customs and Border Protection Program.

d. **USTRANSCOM TCCs** described below and shown in Figure II-1 achieve optimum intermodal capability through integration of common-user transportation systems and resources. Transportation assets remain under the administrative control of the respective Service component commanders. The TCCs continue to perform Service-unique missions, Service-oriented and common-user procurement, training, and maintenance scheduling.

(1) **Air Mobility Command (AMC).** AMC is a major command of the US Air Force. As a transportation component of USTRANSCOM, AMC provides common-user air mobility and aeromedical evacuation transportation services to deploy, employ, sustain, and

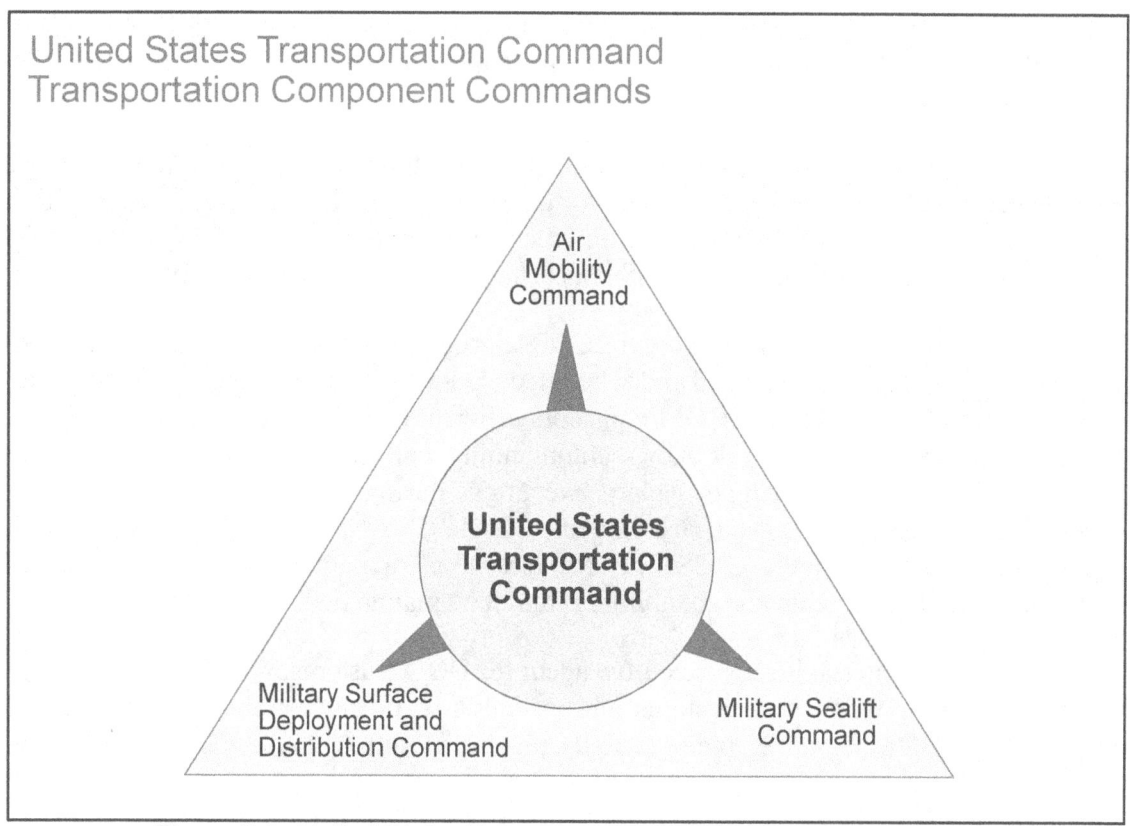

Figure II-1. United States Transportation Command Transportation Component Commands

redeploy US forces on a global basis. Additionally, AMC is the single port manager (SPM) of common-user aerial ports of embarkation (APOEs) and/or aerial ports of debarkation (APODs).

(2) **Military Sealift Command (MSC).** MSC is a major command of the US Navy. As a transportation component of USTRANSCOM, MSC provides common-user and exclusive use sealift transportation services to deploy, employ, sustain, and redeploy US forces on a global basis.

For more information on MSC, refer to JP 4-01.2, Sealift Support to Joint Operations.

(3) **Military Surface Deployment and Distribution Command (SDDC).** SDDC is an operational level Army force designated by the Secretary of the Army as the Army Service Component Command of USTRANSCOM and a major subordinate command of US Army Materiel Command. As a transportation component of USTRANSCOM, SDDC provides worldwide common-use ocean terminal services and traffic management services to deploy, employ, sustain, and redeploy US forces on a global basis. These services include the use of common-user sealift through the Voluntary Intermodal Sealift Agreement (VISA) program. SDDC also conducts transportation engineering to ensure deployability and feasibility of present and future deployment assets. Additionally, SDDC is the SPM for all common-user seaports of embarkation (SPOEs) and seaports of debarkation (SPODs), and manages the Defense Freight Railway Interchange Fleet (DFRIF). When designated (e.g.,

using stevedoring services contracts or host-nation support (HNS), SDDC also serves as the port operator. Surface Deployment and Distribution Command Transportation Engineering Agency (SDDCTEA) provides deployment engineering, research, and analytical expertise to improve the deployability of the Armed Forces of the United States. SDDCTEA executes surface transportation engineering policy matters assigned by the Office of the SecDef on behalf of USTRANSCOM and SDDC headquarters (HQ). SDDCTEA also provides a focal point for developing DTS-related modeling and simulation tools. SDDCTEA's primary functions are to:

(a) Evaluate the highways, railroads, and ports for national defense programs.

(b) Conduct force deployability, transportation infrastructure, and operations and/or exercise analyses.

(c) Assess the capability of power projection platforms and seaports to meet deployment requirements.

(d) Ensure that transportability design influence, criteria, and critical movement considerations are integrated in the DOD acquisition process.

(e) Formulate movement procedures for existing and future material.

(f) Develop deployability analysis techniques and transportation models and simulations, and

(g) Manage the acquisition and distribution of authoritative transportation data in support of deployment requirements.

e. **Geographic Combatant Commanders**

(1) **General.** GCCs, in coordination with CDRUSTRANSCOM and other supporting commanders, are jointly responsible for the deployment of forces from origin to destination.

(2) **Plan Development.** In response to deliberate plan taskings by CJCS, GCCs develop a concept of operations (CONOPS) using the forces and assumptions made available for planning in the JSCP and GEF. Subordinate component commanders then determine their specific force requirements, logistic requirements, and personnel replacements with recommended time phasing. Supported and supporting commanders' planners integrate component requirements and develop the TPFDD, which identifies force requirements to support a particular plan and provides routing data from origin to destination. Within this planning construct, supported and supporting commanders' planners:

(a) Employ factors detailed in TDPs as specified in CJCSI 3110.03, *Logistics Supplement to the Joint Strategic Capabilities Plan,* provide theater mobility and distribution analysis of the infrastructure, support relationships, and customer locations to ensure sufficient capacity or planned enhanced capability. The TDP includes a comprehensive list of references, country data, and information requirements necessary to plan, assess, and conduct theater distribution and joint reception, staging, onward movement, and integration (JRSOI) operations. The TDP also includes theater specific deployment considerations, including primary APODs and SPODs, support for theater organic and common user airlift, and requirements for generating critical enablers.

(b) Analyze movement requirements to determine transportation feasibility using available assets apportioned in the CJCSI 3110.11, *Mobility Supplement to Joint Strategic Capabilities Plan.* After final refinement, the total requirement becomes part of the JOPES database.

(3) **Joint Deployment and Distribution Operations Center (JDDOC).** At time of need a supported GCC can create a JDDOC and incorporate its capabilities into their staff functions. The JDDOC develops deployment and distribution plans, integrates multinational and/or interagency deployment and distribution, and coordinates and synchronizes supply, transportation, and related distribution activities. The JDDOC synchronizes the strategic to operational movement of forces and sustainment into theater by providing advance notice to the GCC's air and surface theater movement C2 elements. In concert with the GCC's overall priorities, and on behalf of the GCC, the JDDOC coordinates common user and theater distribution operations above the tactical level.

For more information, see JP 4-09, Distribution Operations.

(4) **Joint Movement Center (JMC).** A JMC may be established at a subordinate unified or joint task force (JTF) level to coordinate the employment of all means of common-user theater transportation (including that provided by allies, partner nations, or the HN) to support the theater CONOPS. This coordination is accomplished through establishment of theater and JTF transportation policies within the assigned operational area, consistent with relative urgency of need, port and terminal capabilities, transportation asset availability, and priorities set by a JFC. The JTF JMC will work closely with the JDDOC.

(5) **Theater-Joint Transportation Board (T-JTB).** Because transportation is critical to any operation requiring the movement of military forces, CCMDs need the ability to allocate available transportation resources rapidly. Each command should establish allocation procedures during peacetime to facilitate a smooth transition during crisis operations. Therefore, CCDRs should establish a T-JTB to address transportation issues within their command, such as allocating apportioned transportation among components for unit movement, non-unit movement, and resupply. This action should be initiated as close to the beginning of a deployment as possible in order to preclude confusion and backlogs, and to deconflict commercial, US military, and other demands on in-theater transportation assets.

f. **Military Departments and DOD Agencies**

(1) The Military Departments retain the responsibility for organizing, training, equipping, and providing the logistic support (including Service-organic transportation) of their respective forces. These forces and other DOD agencies must depend on common-user military transportation services. In this role, the Army, Navy (including United States Coast Guard [USCG] when appropriate), Air Force, Marine Corps, DLA, and other DOD agencies

are all generically called "shipper services." Each Service is responsible for establishing transportation policy for the movement of equipment and supplies funded by the applicable shipper service and for administrative support and performance of transportation operations assigned by CCDRs at either their local shipping installations or throughout the theater. They are also responsible for maintaining trained personnel that can participate in joint planning and provide JOPES inputs. Each of the Services as well as DLA operate either a joint or Service-specific transportation office that is responsible for requesting transportation through DTS to move household goods, supplies (including ammunition), unit equipment, and military forces or within CONUS, the overseas theater, between CONUS and the overseas theaters, or to support the GCC during routine and crisis generated deployments.

(2) The US Army Corps of Engineers District Engineers, subject to Department of Transportation Emergency Organization (DOTEO) policy direction, perform waterway rehabilitation and construction throughout the US. Except for the Tennessee River System and the St. Lawrence Seaway System, the US Army Corps of Engineers supplies damage assessment data to both the National Resource Analysis Center and DOTEO.

(3) DLA provides worldwide logistic support to the Services, CCMDs, other DOD components, USG departments and agencies, foreign governments, and international organizations.

(4) The National Geospatial-Intelligence Agency provides standard and tailored imagery, imagery intelligence, and geospatial information and services to DOD and other federal organizations. Distribution of standard geospatial products is accomplished by DLA.

(5) Defense Information Systems Agency (DISA), in conjunction with the DOD CIO, provides for planning, developing, and supporting C2 and communications and computer systems that serve the needs of the President and SecDef. It provides guidance and support on technical and operational C2 system issues affecting the Office of the Secretary of Defense, Military Departments, CJCS and the Joint Staff, CCMDs, and DOD agencies. It ensures the interoperability of the GCCS, the Defense Information System Network, theater and tactical C2 systems, North Atlantic Treaty Organization (NATO) and/or allied command, control, and communications systems, and those national and/or international commercial systems that affect the DISA mission. It supports national security emergency preparedness telecommunications functions of the National Communications System.

(6) The Defense Intelligence Agency (DIA) provides transportation intelligence to USTRANSCOM and other DOD commands and agencies during the planning and conduct of military operations.

4. **Department of Transportation**

a. **General.** Under Executive Order 12656, *Assignment of Emergency Preparedness Responsibilities*, the Secretary of Transportation (SECTRANS) leads the federal transportation community. During national defense emergencies, the SECTRANS has a wide range of delegated responsibilities, including executive management of the Nation's transportation resources to meet essential military transportation needs.

(1) The Emergency Transportation Operations (ETO) team is the SECTRANS's peacetime staff element responsible for emergency transportation planning.

(2) The ETO team is responsible for the executive management of civil transportation resources. In anticipation of, or in response to, a national defense-related emergency, the SECTRANS will exercise the delegated authorities of the Defense Priority and Allocation System, as authorized in the Defense Production Act, to provide civil transportation priority (TP) service to DOD before and during mobilization. Under national defense emergency conditions, the SECTRANS will govern the priority use of all civil transportation and the allocation of its capacity to meet essential civil and military needs. Federal transportation agencies will carry out their plans in compliance with SECTRANS policy.

b. **Federal Aviation Administration (FAA).** The FAA is responsible for the following:

(1) Operating national airspace systems and civil air or general aviation transportation facilities, including air traffic control.

(2) Ensuring the safety of commercial aircraft through federal aviation regulations, the establishment of standards, inspections, and the imposition of flight restrictions through circulars and special federal aviation regulations.

(3) Providing priority service orders to support DOD requirements, subject to Department of Transportation (DOT) ETO approval.

(4) Administering Chapter 443 "Aviation War Risk" insurance program for Civil Reserve Air Fleet (CRAF) carriers.

c. **Federal Highway Administration (FHWA).** The FHWA is responsible for administering the Federal-Aid Highway Program. Financial assistance for the construction and improvement of transportation facilities (highways and transit) is made available to state transportation agencies and local governments through several programs, usually by legislative formulas. Individual projects are planned and developed by the state and local governments in accordance with procedures and regulations established by the FHWA, which oversees the program through field offices in each state. The FHWA works closely with SDDC to address defense-related transportation requirements. FHWA, in coordination with the state highway departments, has developed an emergency highway traffic regulation plan. The program becomes operational at the direction of the federal transportation officials.

d. **Federal Railroad Administration (FRA).** The FRA consolidates government support of rail transportation activities, provides national rail policy, administers and enforces rail safety laws and regulations, administers financial assistance programs for railroads, and conducts research and development in support of intercity ground transportation and future requirements for rail transportation. The FRA also provides federal oversight of all Amtrak passenger service.

e. **Maritime Administration (MARAD).** MARAD has primary federal responsibility for ensuring the availability of efficient water transportation service to American shippers and consumers. MARAD seeks to ensure that the United States enjoys adequate shipbuilding and repair service, efficient CONUS ports, effective intermodal water and land transportation systems, and reserve shipping capacity in time of national emergency. MARAD administers federal laws and programs designed to support and maintain a US merchant marine capable of meeting the Nation's shipping needs for both domestic and foreign commerce and national security. MARAD advances the capabilities of the maritime industry to provide total logistic support (port, intermodal, ocean shipping, and training) to the military Services during war or national emergencies through the following:

(1) Maintaining, in accordance with DOD readiness criteria, an active fleet of strategic sealift vessels in the Maritime Administration Ready Reserve Force (MARAD RRF), a component of the inactive National Defense Reserve Fleet (NDRF), to support emergency and national security sealift needs;

(2) Administering funding for the maintenance of the MARAD RRF and NDRF;

(3) Administering the Maritime Security Program (MSP) and the priorities and allocations of the VISA;

(4) Acquiring US flag, US-owned, and other militarily useful merchant ships in accordance with appropriate authorities from the Merchant Marine Act of 1936 and the Emergency Foreign Vessels Acquisition Act of 1954;

(5) Ensuring readiness preparation and coordination of commercial strategic ports for mobilization through the National Port Readiness Network;

(6) Administering the Vessel War Risk Insurance Program (Title 12, United States Code [USC], Merchant Marine Act of 1936); and

(7) Sponsoring merchant mariner training programs for both licensed and unlicensed seamen and ensuring reemployment rights for merchant marines who crew sealift vessels during a sealift crisis.

5. Department of Homeland Security

a. **United States Coast Guard.** The USCG is the primary US maritime agency for waterway safety and security. Port safety responsibilities include the establishment, certification, and supervision of ammunition loading operations and port capability. Upon declaration of war or Presidential direction, the Coast Guard comes under the operational control (OPCON) of the Department of the Navy for port safety and port security responsibilities in both CONUS and outside the continental United States (OCONUS). To ensure the safety and security of CONUS strategic seaports, the Coast Guard chairs the Port Readiness Committee and conducts port readiness exercises. The Coast Guard's role in documenting additional merchant mariners to serve expanded defense shipping needs is integral to the mobilization process.

b. **Customs and Border Protection (CBP).** CBP maintains surveillance of commercial and military terminals for illegal goods and for the improper transfer of United States Munitions List (USML) items. CBP maintains surveillance of agricultural products entering the United States through DTS terminals. It ensures that military equipment returning to the US is free from organisms that could infect and adversely impact the US agriculture and forestry industries.

c. **Federal Emergency Management Agency (FEMA).** FEMA is responsible for preparedness for, response to, and recovery from disasters within the US or US territories.

d. **Transportation Security Administration (TSA).** TSA protects the nation's transportation systems to ensure freedom of movement for people and commerce.

6. Other United States Government Departments and Agencies

a. **Department of Energy (DOE).** DOE ensures crude oil, petroleum products, solid fuels, natural gas, gaseous liquids, and nuclear materials are available and regulates many aspects of their movements.

b. **Department of the Interior (DOI).** DOI, through the Tennessee Valley Authority and in concert with the US Army Corps of Engineers, keeps the Tennessee River System navigable.

c. **Department of Health and Human Services (DHHS).** DHHS has responsibility for receiving, processing, and relocating noncombatant evacuees.

d. **Department of State (DOS).** DOS is responsible for the operation of the noncombatant evacuation program. DOS also coordinates OCONUS overflight rights, diplomatic clearances, and visa and/or passport requirements. The DOS also controls the export and temporary import of defense articles and services contained on the USML through the Directorate of Defense Trade Controls.

e. **US Postal Service (USPS).** USPS is an independent establishment of the Executive Branch of government and maintains movement of essential military mail.

f. **National Oceanic and Atmospheric Administration (NOAA).** The NOAA provides aeronautical data and environmental weather services.

g. **General Services Administration (GSA).** GSA manages government property and records, including construction and operation of buildings, procurement and distribution of supplies, and transportation programs such as the domestic and international city-pairs contract and small package domestic express service contract program. Under the provisions of a strategic partnership with DOD, GSA requires all participants in the city-pairs program to be CRAF members. In return, DOD personnel are mandatory users of the GSA city-pairs domestic and international contracts, as well as the DOD blanket purchase agreement within the GSA domestic express contract. Additionally, GSA authorizes non-DOD agencies to use the USTRANSCOM World Wide Express (WWX) contract.

h. **The Office of United States Foreign Disaster Assistance (OFDA).** OFDA, within the United States Agency for International Development, has primary responsibility for the US response in foreign humanitarian assistance (FHA) operations. OFDA's responsibilities include organizing and coordinating the total USG FHA response to a disaster, performing needs assessment, and initiating procurement of necessary supplies, services, and transportation. OFDA also funds selected relief activities performed by nongovernmental organizations and international organizations OCONUS and in its territories.

i. **USG Departments and Agencies Dealing with Hazardous Materials and Wastes.** USG departments and agencies which DTS interfaces with for the use, storage, and movement of hazardous material and dangerous cargo include the following:

(1) US Environmental Protection Agency;

(2) US Department of Labor-Occupational Safety and Health Administration;

(3) DLA Disposition Services;

(4) National Defense Center for Environmental Excellence;

(5) US Army Environmental Center;

(6) US DOT-Research and Special Programs Administration; and

(7) US DOE.

7. State and Local Transportation Organizations

These organizations consist of levels of government that have responsibility for highway, water (including inland waterway), rail, motor carrier, and/or air transportation.

a. Emergency highway traffic regulations are primarily the responsibility of state highway departments operating under the general supervision and guidance of the regional offices of the FHWA.

b. State and local governments are responsible for the emergency use of in-transit transportation resources, subject to federal policies and national control systems.

c. State and local governments comply with federal control measures to ensure that essential interstate and international movements are not unduly interrupted.

d. These agencies own nearly all public roads and streets (including the interstate system) and are responsible for construction, maintenance, and operation, as well as enforcement of traffic laws. DOD policy stipulates no DOD movement exceeding the legal limitations or regulations of state, local, or toll authorities will occur without proper notification and approval.

8. Commercial Transportation Service Providers

The commercial transportation community has significant capacity to augment DOD and other federal resources. For example, programs such as CRAF and VISA make up a significant portion of US wartime lift capability. Accordingly, the relationship between the civil sector and federal transportation agencies should be strong. Organizations and associations such as the National Defense Transportation Association provide common forums to discuss and endorse programs to promote transportation preparedness and cooperation in peace or war.

CHAPTER III
TRANSPORTATION RESOURCES

"There never is a convenient place to fight a war when the other man starts it."

Arleigh Burke (American Admiral of the United States Navy during World War II and the Korean War, 1901–1996)

1. Purpose

This chapter describes the types of transportation resources available to DOD and explains how these resources are used, activated, and augmented across the range of military operations.

2. Air Mobility

a. **Air Mobility Command. As a TCC of USTRANSCOM**, AMC is the designated lead major command for Air Force air mobility issues and standards and is responsible for all CONUS-based common-user airlift service air mobility assets. USTRANSCOM is responsible for maintaining international air tenders. AMC is responsible for all commercial air tenders and the WWX international commercial express package service contract. AMC C-5, C-17, C-130, KC-10, and KC-135 aircraft are stationed in CONUS and operate through a combination of active, Air Force Reserve, and Air National Guard resources (when mobilized) to provide common-user air mobility under the COCOM of CDRUSTRANSCOM. Additionally, AMC trains, equips, and operates CONUS-gained Air Force C-130s, C-40s, and operational support airlift (OSA) air mobility assets until they are assigned or attached to a GCC. During a contingency or major operation, a number of these short-range aircraft may be attached to a GCC to create or supplement the theater air mobility capability. AMC air mobility forces conduct both intertheater and intratheater common-user operations. Under certain conditions, AMC longer-range aircraft may be temporarily deployed to a GCC's area of responsibility (AOR), even if only on a mission-by-mission basis, to provide additional theater capability. See Figure III-1 for a graphic representation of air mobility resources.

b. **Geographic CCMDs**. GCCs exercise COCOM over assigned air mobility forces and either OPCON or tactical control over attached air mobility forces. These forces could include C-130s, C-17s, KC-10s, KC-135s, C-40s, or Service OSA aircraft such as C-21s or C-12s. The inventory of these aircraft is dependent on documented requirements validated by CJCS.

c. **Air Reserve Component (ARC)**. Air Force Reserve and Air National Guard units operating C-5, C-17, KC-10, most KC-135, and most C-130 aircraft mobilize under AMC. Air National Guard forces are normally under the peacetime C2 of the states' governors. GCCs exercise OPCON of ARC forces (less intertheater mobility forces assigned to USTRANSCOM) on active duty for either training or performing inactive-duty training within their AORs (except in CONUS, Hawaii, Alaska, Puerto Rico, or US territories), or participating anywhere in military operations or joint training under their jurisdiction. As a

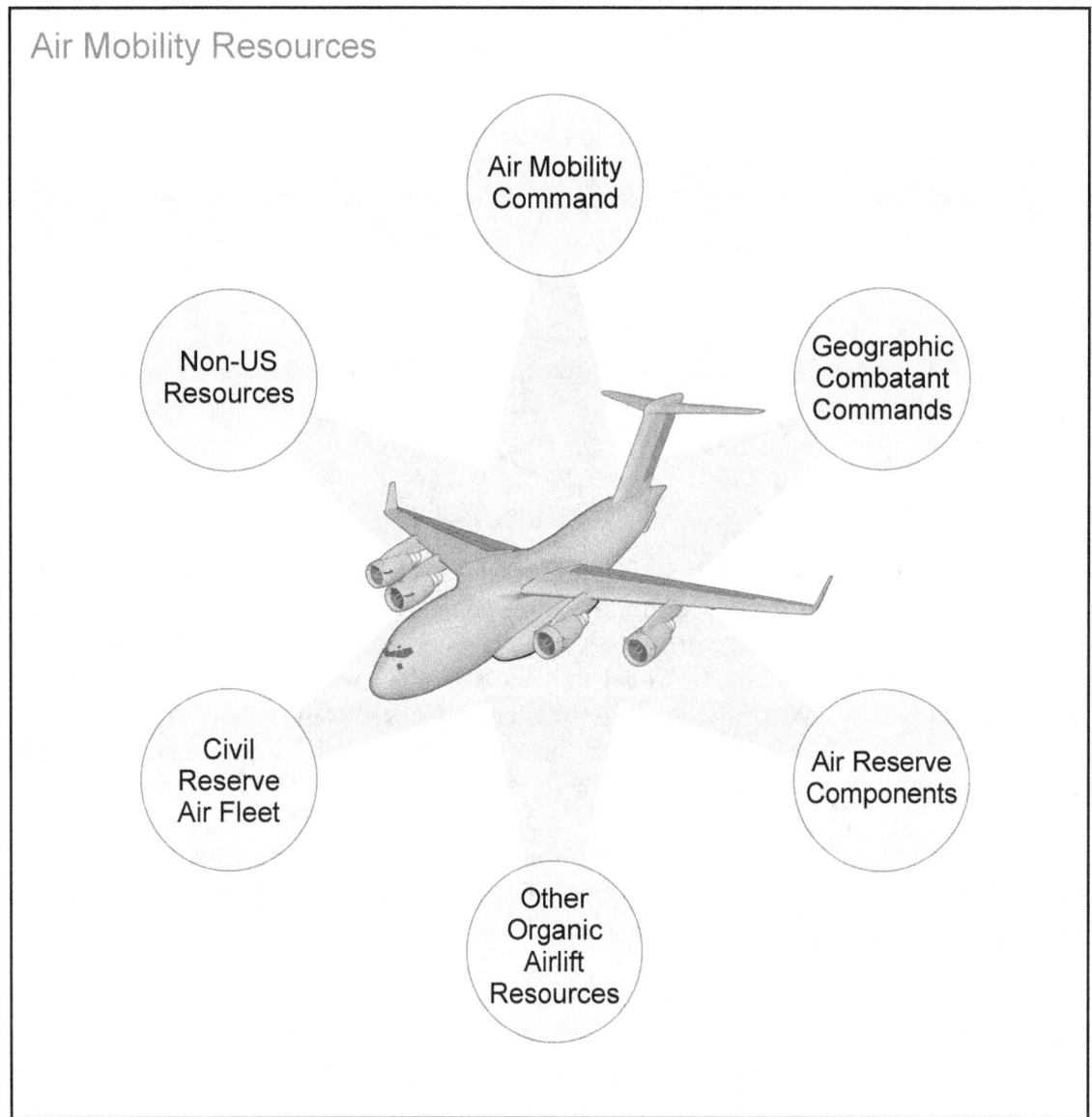

Figure III-1. Air Mobility Resources

matter of DOD policy, CCDRs may exercise training and readiness oversight authority for assigned ARC forces when not on active duty or when on active duty for training. CCDRs exercise COCOM over assigned ARC forces only when they are mobilized or ordered to active duty. To facilitate training, ARC units volunteer aircraft and aircrews to AMC in peacetime for short-term missions. They provide logistic air mobility support between the US (including the territories) and the other theaters, participate in CJCS exercises, and provide rotational capabilities for theater requirements. The ARC also provides OSA capability to the CCDRs and Services.

d. **Operational Support Airlift (OSA).** OSA is a special classification mission to provide for the timely movement of limited numbers of priority personnel and cargo during wartime, as well as peacetime training for pilots and priority airlift for key decision makers. OSA operations tend to be conducted by smaller-sized business type airframes. While OSA

Air mobility resources are vital to the rapid movement of personnel and cargo.

operations are normally conducted either in direct support of the assigned organization's organic requirements or pooled at the CCMD level, OSA assets may be used to reduce extraordinary workload demands on the air mobility system. USTRANSCOM is responsible for scheduling OSA missions with CONUS-based assets while the Services validate OSA requests. GCCs with their own OSA fleets are responsible for scheduling and execution tasking of OSA operations within their AORs.

    e. **Service Organic Air Mobility Resources.** Service organic air mobility forces are those assets that are an integral part of a specific Service, component, or major command and primarily support the requirements of the organization to which they are assigned. Air mobility planners should coordinate the use of excess Service organic mobility assets made available for common-user missions.

    f. **Civil Reserve Air Fleet.** CRAF is designed to augment DOD capability with contractually committed US civil aircraft, aircrews, and support structure when requirements exceed DOD air mobility capability and voluntary support is either insufficient or unavailable. CRAF aircraft are not designed to carry most oversized and outsized cargo. Additionally, these aircraft may require special handling and loading equipment.

    (1) CRAF is comprised of two segments: the international segment and the national segment (see Figure III-2).

    (a) **International Segment.** This segment consists of long-range and short-range sections. The long-range section provides the largest capability with passenger and

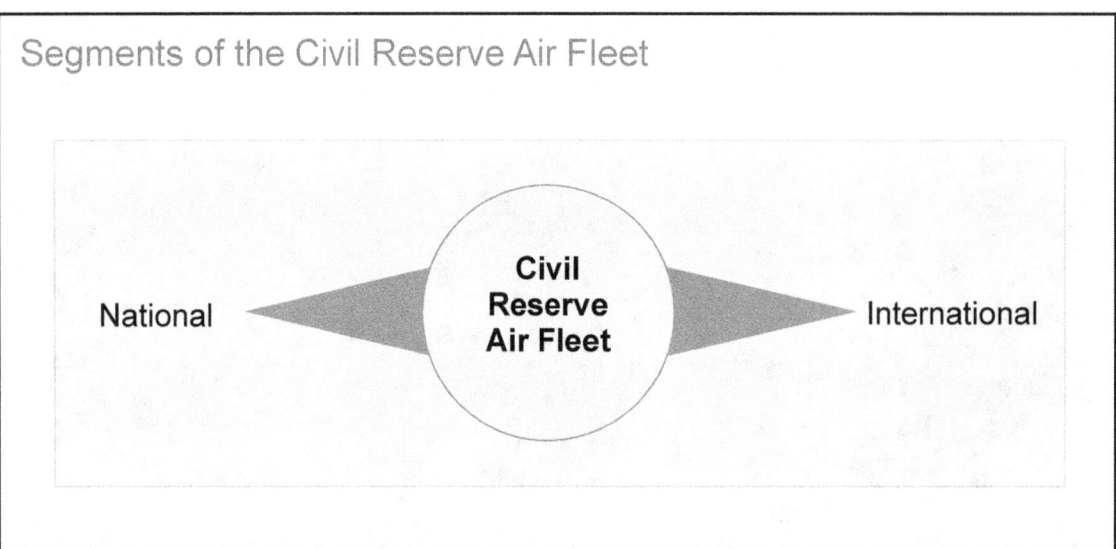

Figure III-2. Segments of the Civil Reserve Air Fleet

cargo aircraft. Aircraft must be extended-range capable (over water). The short-range section supports near offshore operations with both passenger and cargo aircraft.

(b) **National Segment.** This segment consists of the domestic services and Alaska sections. The domestic services section provides passenger and cargo aircraft for domestic-only service using regional US air carriers with at least 75 seats (30,000 pounds allowable cabin load) and a cargo capability of at least 32,000 pounds. The domestic services section is used in CRAF Stages II and III. The Alaska section provides cargo aircraft support to Alaska in CRAF Stages II and III.

(2) With the approval of SecDef, CDRUSTRANSCOM activates CRAF in response to defense-oriented situations (up to and including a declared national emergency or war) to satisfy DOD airlift requirements. The activation of the CRAF can be tailored to meet varying levels of defense air mobility requirements. The CRAF can be activated all at once or incrementally by type of capability needed (passenger, cargo, etc.) and amount of capacity needed. Although AMC assumes mission control of CRAF airlift assets during activation, individual CRAF carriers retain responsibility for their own assets. In this way, the US military gains use of civil aircraft and aircrews and access to their en route support structure. The three stages of CRAF organized to meet the varying levels of defense airlift requirements are as follows:

(a) **CRAF Stage I, Committed Expansion.** This stage involves DOD use of civil air carrier resources to support substantially expanded peacetime military airlift requirements. This stage supports minor regional crises or small-scale contingencies.

(b) **CRAF Stage II, Defense Airlift Emergency.** This stage involves DOD use of civil air resources and air carriers to furnish to DOD in time of a defense airlift emergency. This stage supports major regional conflicts or a major theater war.

The Civil Reserve Air Fleet is used to augment military air mobility capabilities in times of national emergency.

(c) **CRAF Stage III, National Emergency.** This stage involves use of civil air resources owned by a US entity or citizen air carriers furnished to DOD in time of declared national defense-oriented emergency or war, or when otherwise necessary for the national defense. This stage supports multiple theaters of war and national mobilization.

For additional information on CRAF and its activation stages, see JP 3-17, Air Mobility Operations.

g. **Non-US Resources.** Airlift capacity is also available from foreign allies and NATO entities via cooperative military airlift agreements, acquisition and cross-servicing agreements (ACSAs), and similar arrangements. Foreign flag air carriers may also be used in some circumstances. However, the use of any foreign flag air carrier is subject to the Fly America and the Fly CRAF Acts. In addition, any foreign air carrier used for the charter air transportation of US military passengers and cargo must have been approved for DOD use by the DOD Commercial Airlift Review Board.

3. Sealift

Shipping resources can be classified into three pools: USG-owned, US flag commercial, and foreign flag commercial assets.

a. **USG-Owned Assets.** DOD (MSC) maintains a fleet of operating organic vessels as well as a fleet in a reduced operating status (ROS). DOT (MARAD) maintains a fleet of vessels in a ROS that can be turned over to MSC to operate during a contingency.

(1) **Military Sealift Command.** In peacetime, MSC is responsible for operating assigned organic vessels and for awarding and implementing contracts with commercial charter operators to meet DOD lift requirements. Today the organic fleet is comprised primarily of nine large, medium-speed roll-on/roll-off (LMSR) surge vessels; MSC also operates six additional pre-positioning LMSRs available for common-user lift requirements once their wartime stocks are downloaded. During a contingency, MSC is responsible for recommending and executing a number of DOD and commercial sealift programs. When directed by CDRUSTRANSCOM, MSC may initially use the DOD and MARAD fleets, as well as those under treaty agreements. If that proves to be insufficient, MSC may solicit commercial capacity through volunteers or by executing contingency contracts MSC maintains with their commercial partners.

(a) **Surge Sealift Ships. This fleet consists of dry cargo, tankers, and LMSRs.** The majority of this fleet consists of nine LMSRs that are strategically layberthed near ports on the West, Gulf, and East Coasts of the US. All are in four-day ROS-4 and capable of carrying over 300,000 square feet of heavy wheeled vehicles and rotary aircraft at sustained speeds of 24 knots.

(b) **Pre-Positioning Ships.** DOD positions a number of vessels around the world that are loaded with equipment and material required to respond rapidly to the full range of military operations; from major combat operations, to theater security cooperation, to humanitarian assistance and disaster relief. All of the DOD Services maintain several of these vessels. Details on this fleet can be found in paragraph 7, "Pre-Positioning and Forward Stocking."

(2) **The Maritime Administration.** MARAD is the DOT's agency responsible for administering federal laws and programs designed to support and maintain a US merchant marine capable of meeting the Nation's needs. It is responsible by law for the management of the NDRF. A key component of the NDRF is the MARAD RRF, which is maintained by MARAD using National Defense Sealift Funds appropriated by DOD. MARAD is also a key organization in the processes for acquiring shipping once the voluntary charter market is no longer responsive.

(3) **The MARAD RRF** consists of commercial or former military vessels of high military utility including fast sealift ships (FSSs), roll-on/roll-off (RO/RO), heavy lift float-on/float-off, petroleum tankers, crane ships, and other unique platforms required by the warfighter to meet their missions. Some of these vessels have had their military capabilities enhanced with additional systems such as the offshore petroleum discharge system (OPDS), which pumps millions of gallons of fuel from sea-to-shore, and the large vessel interface— lift-on/lift-off stabilized crane system which is capable of loading/unloading other vessels at sea while in moderate sea states. MARAD maintains these vessels in ROS- 5 and MARAD RRF-10, 20- or 30-day readiness when not activated and in the custody of MSC for OPCON. MARAD maintains administrative control at all times.

b. **US Flag Fleet.** Ships operating under a US flag are routinely chartered by MSC to meet both long-term and unique government shipping demands. Additionally, universal service contracts are negotiated by USTRANSCOM for government cargo that does not have to move on dedicated charter vessels. When an expansion of USG requirements occurs such that organic and voluntary US and foreign flag shipping can no longer provide sufficient lift capacity, DOD may elect to activate prenegotiated agreements with US flag vessels. There are four acquisition processes, including voluntary chartering, available for DOD acquisition of additional US flag shipping. They are the VISA, the Voluntary Tanker Agreement (VTA), liner service, and requisitioning.

(1) **Voluntary Intermodal Sealift Agreement.** VISA is DOD's primary sealift mobilization program. All major US flag carriers are enrolled and more than 90 percent of the US flag dry cargo fleet is covered under its contingency commitments. It is an intermodal capacity-oriented program vice a ship-by-ship contract, which means when activated DOD is requesting a percentage of a company's total capacity. The purpose of VISA is to provide a coordinated, seamless transition from peacetime to wartime for the acquisition of commercial sealift and related global intermodal services required to augment DOD's sealift capabilities.

(a) VISA is activated upon approval of SecDef and consists of three stages. Stage I is activated by CDRUSTRANSCOM, upon notification to SecDef, when voluntary capacity commitments are insufficient to meet DOD requirements and provides limited access to 15 percent of all Stage 1 enrolled capacity. Stage II is activated in the same way and provides up to 40 percent of all Stage I and Stage II commitments. Stage III is slightly different and requires written approval from SecDef and concurrence from the SECTRANS to allocate up to 50 percent of all Stage I, II, and III capacities based on DOD requirements. In addition, a subset of VISA vessels enrolled under a stand-alone program called the MSP guarantees access to 100 percent of enrolled vessels once stage III is activated. In total, VISA provides an immense capability and ready access to over 160,000 20-foot equivalent units of container capacity, 5.5 million square feet for rolling stock, and 72,000 measurement tons for heavy lift requirements.

(b) A joint planning advisory group (JPAG) is central to the successful implementation of VISA and is comprised of representatives from USTRANSCOM, SDDC, MSC, DLA, MARAD, and intermodal industrial transportation representatives. The JPAG provides USTRANSCOM and its components with recommendations on how to best resolve critical transportation issues during periods of heavy demand or crisis.

(2) **Voluntary Tanker Agreement.** The VTA is a method of acquiring additional petroleum product carriers once the commercial market is no longer responsive. It is a cooperative effort by industry and government to meet military requirements for liquid cargo carriers. It is activated by MARAD at the request of SecDef.

(3) **Liner Service.** USTRANSCOM arranges for common-user ocean services by either establishing new contracts or utilizing existing contracts (universal service contracts or regional delivery contracts) with commercial carriers offering liner service on scheduled trade routes. The liner service established by these contracts may be for container or break bulk service responding to either unit or sustainment requirements.

(4) **Requisitioning.** The last resort for acquisition of shipping is requisitioning. US flag ships—and some vessels owned by US citizens but registered under effectively controlled flag of convenience—may be requisitioned under the authority of Section 902 of the Merchant Marine Act of 1936 (Title 46, USC, Section 1242). Only the President of the United States may authorize requisitioning.

c. **Foreign Flag Ships.** When US flag ships are unavailable, foreign flag ships can be acquired for DOD use through three different methods: voluntary charter, allied shipping agreements, and requisitioning of effective US control shipping.

(1) **Voluntary Charter.** During peacetime, MSC will charter foreign flag ships whenever US flag ships are unavailable. This ability allows MSC to enter the foreign charter market and quickly expand its fleet whenever the need arises.

(2) **Allied Shipping Agreements.** Allied shipping agreements, arranging for vessels received through allied nations, can either be pre-negotiated and in existence or they can be drawn up on an emergency basis as the need arises. An example of these types of agreements is the Korean Flag Shipping Agreement.

(3) **Effective United States-Controlled Ships (EUSCS).** EUSCS are ships owned by US citizens or companies that are registered in countries that have no prohibition on requisitioning of these vessels by the US. These ships may be requisitioned by the US under authority of Section 902, Merchant Marine Act of 1936 (Title 46, USC, Section 1242).

4. Land

a. **Military Surface Deployment and Distribution Command.** SDDC maintains transportation agreements and all commercial carrier costing information necessary to move shipments within the US via surface transportation. This includes approving commercial carriers to conduct business with the DOD; evaluating carrier performance; and maintaining carrier tender information. SDDC obtains rates from commercial carriers through the voluntary tender process and one-time-only rate negotiations. The voluntary tender process allows DOD-approved carriers to submit rates to SDDC, at any time and for any type of move. One-time-only negotiations are performed to obtain rates for specialized moves that are not compatible with voluntary tenders, primarily for rail, barge, unit moves, and shipments with unique requirements.

b. **Defense Freight Railway Interchange Fleet.** SDDC owns and manages the DFRIF. The DFRIF is composed of all cars purchased by, or in-leased on behalf of any branch of the armed forces for loaded movement by commercial railroads throughout North America. The DFRIF is different from the railroad cars that are owned by the individual Services for installation support, principally at ammunition plants, shipyards, and ports. Unlike these cars, DFRIF cars must be constructed to railroad-approved designs, registered with the railroads, and maintained in accordance with railroad rules and federal regulations. The DFRIF is managed as a separate Transportation Working Capital Fund account. The principal revenue source is in payments that the railroads make, in varying amounts depending on the type, cost, and age of a particular car, for each mile that the cars move under load. A secondary

The specialized flat railway cars of the Defense Freight Railway Interchange Fleet are deployable service assets under the control of United States Transportation Command.

source of revenue is rentals from out-leasing, principally from freight forwarders moving foreign military sales equipment to ports. The principal expense category is maintenance, which is performed by the railroads and by three geographically dispersed private car shops under long-term contract to DFRIF. Special purpose cars are built to a unique design to meet the needs of an individual Service; their purchase or in-lease is funded by that Service. Once they are accepted from the manufacturer, ownership and responsibility for maintenance of the cars is transferred to SDDC. The purchaser controls the use of special purpose cars, including whether SDDC may make the cars available for the use of another Service or for out-lease. The Army has the responsibility of funding the purchase of general-purpose cars, which are cars of a design suitable for use by more than one Service. SDDC controls the use of general-purpose cars. Most of the general-purpose flat cars are assigned to specific Army and Marine Corps installations to support mobilization. They are designed to carry containers and wheeled or tracked vehicles. The remaining cars are not assigned to any particular installation and are dispatched as needed to support peacetime traffic. General-purpose tank cars are all used for fuel movements and are divided into pools assigned to specific loading points.

c. **CONUS Commercial Resources.** The commercial transportation industry has substantial capability available to meet the CONUS transportation needs of DOD. SDDC administers the Contingency Response Program (CORE) which supports the acquisition of domestic civil transportation resources during military deployments. This voluntary program provides DOD commercial transportation service support and priority for commercial transportation prior to and during contingency and mobilization. CORE supports resource acquisition for commercial transportation, coordinates hazardous materials movement, acquisition for commercial transportation, coordinates hazardous materials movement, provides liaison to the USCG for port security support, and performs source identification for emergency lease or purchase of commercial heavy equipment transporters.

d. **Defense Transportation Coordination Initiative (DTCI).** DTCI is a joint USTRANSCOM, DLA, and Services program which, under SDDC oversight, uses a commercial third-party logistics provider to manage freight movements in CONUS. This relationship leverages the best in commercial capabilities for more efficient and economic delivery, primarily through visibility of freight movements which enables load consolidation, increased use of intermodal solutions and intelligent scheduling. The use of a single commercial coordinator also assists with the facilitation and generation of relevant and precise metrics collection which in turn drives process improvement.

e. **OCONUS Common-User Land Transportation (CULT).** Assigning responsibility for CULT is a function of the GCC's directive authority for logistics, and it is up to each GCC to outline this in the operation plan (OPLAN) and supporting plans. Under CULT, land transportation assets are normally under the OPCON of the Army component commander, who coordinates all planning and requirements for the use of DOD-controlled land transportation equipment and facilities designated common-use in theater. Service component commanders, however, maintain control and authority over their Service-owned assets that are not designated as common-use to facilitate accomplishment of their mission. The Navy and Air Force components provide organic land transportation support within their installations and activities and submit peacetime requirements for common-use theater or area transportation to the Army component for those theaters where the Army has been assigned CULT responsibility. Wartime CULT requirements are the GCC's responsibility and normally the JDDOC or a component assigned the CULT mission will consolidate and coordinate planned wartime movement requirements for all component commands. Nonmilitary transportation resources can include HNS, multinational civil organizations, indigenous commercial transportation providers, and third party logistic organizations.

5. Theater

There are numerous transportation and mobility resources available to GCCs. The type and number of sources vary by theater.

a. **Supporting and/or Supported Combatant Commander Theater Requirements.** The only source of organic resources to US forces in overseas areas consists of air and surface units assigned to the GCC for common-user transportation service. Common-user transportation assets within the DTS are under the COCOM of CDRUSTRANSCOM, excluding Service-organic or theater-assigned assets. Theater-assigned common-user transportation assets are under the COCOM of the respective GCC. The Air Force and Army component commanders are normally delegated OPCON of their respective Service assets in order to meet common theater requirements. For transportation purposes, supported organizations define movement requirements—what, where, and when. Supporting organizations have resources and responsibility to provide movement capability and are, as such, "supporting."

(1) The supported GCC controls intratheater movement. Theater movement control plans should provide the GCC with the highest practicable degree of influence or control over movement into, within, and out of the theater. Regardless of the option selected, the theater movement control system must allow the GCC the capability to plan, apportion, allocate, coordinate, deconflict movement requirements, and track forces and materiel in the theater. Moreover, the theater movement control plan must coordinate incoming strategic movements with the TDP and theater JRSOI operations.

(2) The supported GCC may decide to control distribution through the logistics directorate of a joint staff (J-4) at the CCMD level tailored and augmented as appropriate, or the GCC may decide to control joint distribution through a subordinate organization. In the latter instance, the GCC will delineate the authorities and command relationships that will be used by the subordinate commander to control distribution. However, to facilitate a fully coordinated and responsive transportation system, the GCC may assign responsibility for theater transportation movement control to the JDDOC or JMC. The control function assigned must be equipped with sufficient communication and automation capabilities to allow adequate interface between intertheater and intratheater transportation systems and the GCC's staff. Whichever organization is assigned, it must be skilled in coordinating and directing theater transportation operations in support of unit movements and sustainment operations.

(3) The GCC has a wide range of movement control options available to allow a seamless intertheater-intratheater interface. Subordinate JFCs or Service components may be directed to carry out their own movement control. However, to facilitate a fully coordinated and responsive transportation system, the GCC may assign responsibility for theater transportation movement control to the JDDOC. The JDDOC must be equipped with sufficient communication and automation capabilities to allow adequate interface between intertheater and intratheater transportation systems and the GCC's staff. This organization must be skilled in coordinating and directing theater transportation operations in support of unit movements and sustainment operations. The GCC's logistic staff normally forms the nucleus of a movement control organization, but a properly executed theater movement control mission requires an additional predesignated augmentation to function as a joint organization. Ideally, such an organization would be identified as a force deployment option in an OPLAN and be established early in the theater to coordinate arrival, theater expansion, and operations movement planning and execution.

(4) All Services have organic capability to execute theater opening functions, among other logistic tasks such as port opening and distribution. Additionally, USTRANSCOM has joint task force–port opening (JTF-PO), which can provide a short-duration joint expeditionary capability to rapidly establish and initially operate an APOD/SPOD.

For more information on Service capabilities and JTF-PO, see JP 4-09, Distribution Operations.

b. **Host-Nation Support.** A frequently used means of augmenting or expanding the GCC's transportation capability is HNS. HNS, negotiated through bilateral or multilateral agreements, provides for a nation to either accept responsibility for a particular function within its borders (e.g., APOD cargo clearance) or designate civilian and/or military resources to be used in that capacity under military control. HNS offers the GCC a proven means to meet theater transportation requirements and offset force structure shortfalls.

c. **Managing Acquisition and Cross-Servicing Agreements (ACSAs).** Negotiated on a bilateral basis usually with multinational partners and sometimes with other eligible countries, ACSAs allow for the exchange of logistic support, supplies, and services during combined exercises, training deployments, operations, and for unforeseen circumstances and contingencies. Some examples include: food, billeting, clothing, communication services, medical services, spare parts and components, training services, petroleum, oils, and lubricants (POL), transportation (including airlift), ammunition and, in limited cases, other items of military equipment.

(1) **Purpose of Program**

(a) Adds flexibility in filling logistic shortfalls during exercises, contingencies, or peculiar situations.

(b) Utilizes other nation's supplies or services or provides the same to a requesting country.

(2) **Methods of Recoupment**

(a) "Repayment in cash" is a cash repayment for parts and/or services. Rates are based on reciprocal pricing.

(b) "Equal value exchange" provides for the payment via an unlike service or part but of equal cash value to what was originally provided (negotiated and agreed prior to transaction).

(c) "Replacement in kind" provides that the user return an identical item to that which was borrowed.

(3) **Program Limitations**

(a) ACSAs are not to be used to procure goods and services reasonably available from US commercial sources.

(b) Military-to-military exchange only.

(c) Title 10, USC, mandates that all ACSA transactions are reimbursed.

(d) All transactions revert to cash if not completed within 365 days from time of service or exchange.

(e) Orders are only requests. The final decision to fulfill a request lies with the actual provider.

(f) Provider absorbs the cost until the user repays with cash, services, and/or parts.

(4) **ACSA Order Process**

(a) ACSA implementing arrangements specify the national office for coordinating ACSA requests.

(b) The request is reviewed by the designated point of contact (POC), who sources the request to the applicable authority and provider.

(c) If agreed, ACSA POCs will coordinate with functional areas and provide instructions for the transaction and the financial procedures.

(5) **CCDRs may negotiate and conclude ACSAs when authorized by CJCS.** The CCDR typically negotiates ACSAs during peacetime, or the responsibility may be delegated to a Service component commander. The Service component is responsible for executing the ACSA. Governed by legal guidelines, ACSAs are to be used for contingencies or exercises to correct logistic deficiencies that cannot be adequately corrected by national means or when convenience and/or economies of scale are desired. The office of primary responsibility for ACSA is the CCDR's plans directorate of a joint staff (J-5).

d. **Multinational civil transportation support organizations and structures** offer yet another source of support for GCCs. These are most developed in the European theater where NATO has peacetime planning organizations, crisis management organizations, and other organizations that are activated during wartime.

e. **Commercial Ocean Carriers.** Under SDDC container agreements, commercial ocean carriers often have an existing infrastructure in developed areas that can transport containerized cargo from SPOD to designated destinations. The theater traffic manager in concert with SDDC can use these services to ease demands on military and HNS assets. However, the theater traffic manager must ensure the release and return of container assets under terms of the container agreement to obtain maximum system efficiency.

f. **Contracted Support Operations.** Contracted support operations can provide additional resources to GCCs when they are properly coordinated with intratheater transportation policies, requirements, and contingency procedures. C2 of the movement of materiel arriving in, and departing from, a theater on commercially contracted assets must be fully integrated into the commander's OPLAN to ensure that transportation requirements are met and to offset transportation force structure shortfalls. Fully integrated OPLANs should address contracted support contractual compliance with DOD policies regarding CRAF and/or VISA participation, contingency validation procedures, TPFDD procedures, ITV, and coordination of civilian operations within DTS. Proper contracted support integration will enable timely movement coordination, transportation assets validation, and required ITV of vital support requirements while easing demands on limited space and essential cargo or materials handling equipment (MHE).

A CRITICAL LINK IN THE DEFENSE TRANSPORTATION SYSTEM

Joint logistics over-the-shore (JLOTS) are operations in which Navy and Army logistics over-the-shore (LOTS) forces conduct LOTS operations together under a joint force commander. JLOTS operations allow US strategic sealift ships to discharge off-shore or in-stream through inadequate or damaged ports, or over a bare beach. JLOTS watercraft can also be used to operationally reposition units and materials within a theater.

For more information on JLOTS, see Joint Publication 4-01.6, *Joint Logistics Over-the-Shore Operations.*

---

6. Port Operations

a. **General.** Military and commercial ports are critical components of DTS supporting the air and maritime movement of unit- and non-unit personnel, equipment, and cargo. These ports could be owned and operated by SDDC, AMC, a Service, GCC, or commercial or HN authorities. They may be either sophisticated fixed locations or heavily dependent on deployable mission support forces or joint logistics over-the-shore (JLOTS) assets to accomplish the mission. The significant surface and air cargo handling capabilities that exist in the Services should be used jointly rather than in isolation to maximize the throughput capability of these essential transportation nodes.

b. The extensive use of containers and 463L pallets makes container-handling equipment (CHE) and MHE essential elements of DTS. Ensuring that these assets are available early allows for the efficient loading and unloading of ships and aircraft and increases the rate at which a port can be cleared.

c. **Single Port Manager.** The SPM performs those functions necessary to support the strategic flow of deploying and redeploying forces, unit equipment, and sustainment supply in the SPOEs and APOEs and hand-off to the GCC in the SPODs and APODs. DOD uses the SPM approach for all worldwide common-use aerial and seaport operations. As outlined in the UCP, USTRANSCOM has the mission to provide worldwide common-user aerial and seaport terminal management and may provide terminal services by contract. Thus USTRANSCOM, through AMC and SDDC, will manage common-use aerial ports and seaports for the GCC. In areas not served by a permanent USTRANSCOM presence, USTRANSCOM deploys an AMC contingency response force and an SDDC port management cell to manage the ports in concert with a designated port operator.

(1) **Surface Deployment and Distribution Command.** SDDC performs SPM functions necessary to support the strategic flow of the deploying forces' equipment and sustainment supply in the SPOE and hand-off to the GCC in the SPOD. SDDC has port management responsibility through all phases of the theater port operations continuum, from a bare beach (e.g., JLOTS) deployment to a commercial contract fixed-port support deployment. When necessary, in areas where SDDC does not maintain a manned presence, a deployment support team will be established to direct water terminal operations, including supervising movement operations, contracts, cargo documentation, CONUS security

---

operations, arranging for support, and the overall flow of information. As the seaport SPM, SDDC is also responsible for providing strategic deployment status information to the CCDR and managing the workload of the SPOD port operator based on the CCDR's priorities and guidance. SDDC transportation groups and other SDDC units operate ports that use contracted labor. If Army stevedores are used, transportation groups assigned to the CCDR operate the port.

The specific roles and functions of both the port manager and port operator are summarized in JP 4-01.5, Joint Terminal Operations.

(2) **Air Mobility Command.** AMC performs SPM functions necessary to support the strategic flow of the deploying forces' equipment and sustainment supply in the APOE and hand-off to the GCC in the APOD. AMC has port management responsibility through all phases of the theater aerial port operations continuum, from a bare base deployment to a commercial contract fixed-port support deployment. AMC is the single aerial port manager and, where designated, operator of common-user APOEs and/or APODs.

For additional information, see JP 4-01.5, Joint Terminal Operations.

7. Pre-Positioning and Forward Stocking

a. **Pre-Positioning.** DOD pre-positioned force, equipment, or supplies (PREPO) programs (see Figure III-3) are both land- and sea-based. They are critical programs for reducing closure times of combat and support forces needed in the early stages of a contingency. They also contribute significantly to reducing demands on DTS. The US Army and US Marine Corps pre-positioning programs consist of combat and combat support or sustainment capabilities, to include in-stream discharge and JLOTS capabilities. Other Service and DLA PREPO programs are logistics oriented.

(1) PREPO operations require a permissive security environment. Therefore, the potential region of crisis must be identified in advance and areas for receiving, issuing, and staging PREPO must be made secure.

(2) Pre-positioned equipment requires varying degrees of preparation prior to issue to deploying forces. Equipment stored for years in climate-controlled ships, and warehouses will require depreservation, calibration, and some maintenance effort. Services dispatch advance parties to perform maintenance, offload and/or issue, and staging functions.

(3) The issue and receipt of pre-positioned materiel occurs during the Joint Deployment Process. Planning factors for successful PREPO operations include having; a permissive environment to receive and/or issue, stage, and move pre-positioned equipment forward; sufficient APODs to receive deploying forces; suitable real estate and transportation infrastructure to stage and onward move PREPO; and sufficient in-theater logistic, force protection, C2, communications system, and intelligence support. Finally, when afloat PREPO stocks are needed, sufficient SPOD facilities must be made available to receive afloat PREPO ships. Once PREPO vessels are discharged, the CCDR can release OPCON of them to MSC for common-user service.

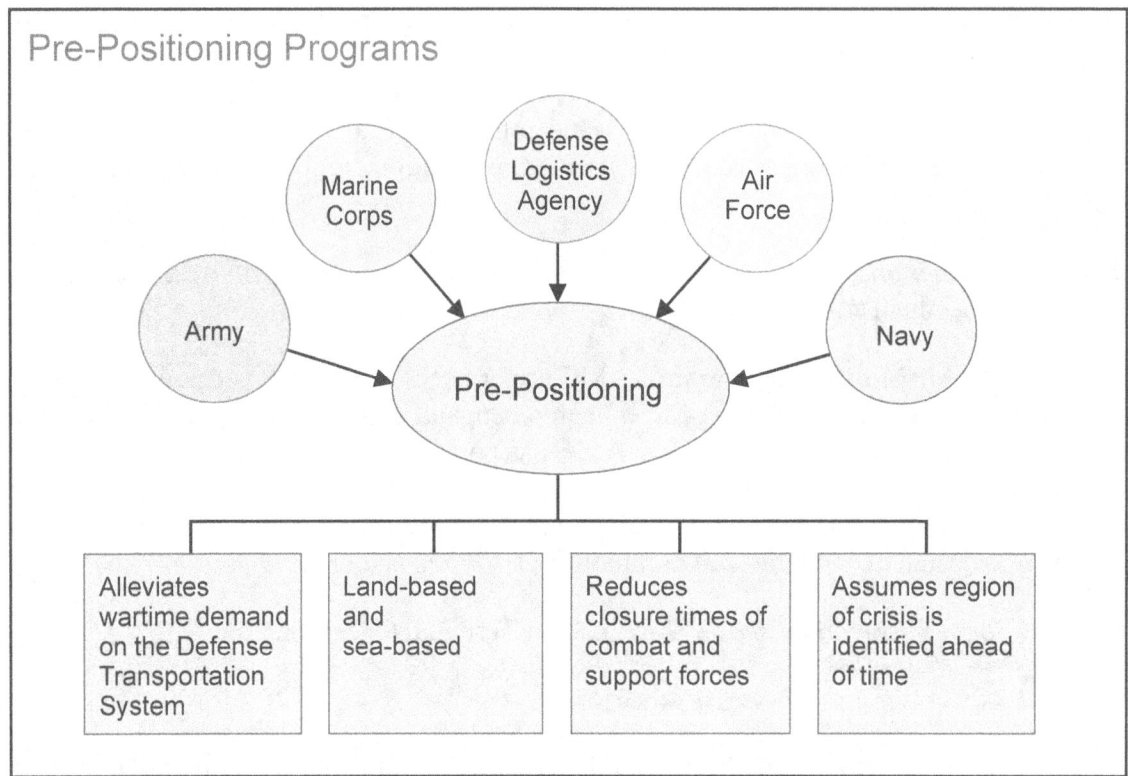

Figure III-3. Pre-Positioning Programs

For more information on JRSOI, see JP 3-35, Deployment and Redeployment Operations.

(4) **Afloat Pre-Positioning Force (APF).** In addition to sealift ships, MSC operates the APF, a fleet of pre-positioned ships strategically placed around the world and loaded with equipment and supplies to sustain Army, Marine Corps, Air Force, and DLA operations. These ships are chartered commercial and government-owned vessels and remain at sea, ready to deploy on short notice. The APF consists of maritime pre-positioning ships (MPSs), Army pre-positioned stocks (APS) ships, and DLA, and Air Force ships.

(5) **US Army.** The Army maintains the APS program. The primary purpose of APS is to reduce the time needed to assemble a force of sufficient size and capability to support the GCC's OPLAN. Accordingly, APS are located at several land-based locations, as well as aboard ships, to quickly project power to contingency areas. APS can be approved for release by CJCS and/or the GCC, while the shore-based Army PREPO can be released by CJCS, Chief of Staff of the Army, or Department of the Army designated personnel. APS has both land and sea components. APS are designated APS-1, APS-3, APS-4, and APS-5. With the exception of APS-1 that consists of sustainment materiel and operational projects (OPROJs) stored in CONUS, all other APS sets are land-based OCONUS or afloat, and possess robust combat and sustainment capabilities.

(a) **Pre-Positioned Unit Sets.** Equipment, configured into unit sets (to include authorized stockage list, prescribed load list, and unit basic load), is positioned ashore and afloat in order to reduce deployment response times by meeting the Army's Global

Pre-Positioning Strategy requirements to provide simultaneous support to more than one contingency in more than one theater.

(b) **Operational Project Stocks.** OPROJ stocks consist of materiel above normal table of organization and equipment, table of distribution and allowances, and common table of allowance authorizations tailored to key strategic capabilities essential to the Army's ability to execute its force projection strategy. OPROJ stocks are designed to support one or more Army operations, plans, or contingencies.

(c) **Army War Reserve Sustainment Stocks.** The Army procures sustainment stocks in peacetime to meet increased wartime requirements. They consist of major and secondary materiel designated to satisfy the Army's wartime sustainment requirements. They provide minimum essential support to combat operations and post-mobilization training beyond the capabilities of peacetime stocks, industry, and HNS. Army War Reserve Sustainment Stocks are pre-positioned in or near a theater of operations to be used until wartime production and supply lines can be established. These stocks consist of major end items to sustain the operation by replacing combat losses consumed in the operation.

(d) **War Reserve Stocks for Allies (WRSA).** WRSA is a program directed by the Office of the Secretary of Defense and facilitates US preparedness to assist designated allies in case of war. WRSA assets are pre-positioned in the appropriate theater and owned and financed by the US. They are released to the appropriate Army component commander for transfer to the supported multinational force under provisions in the Foreign Assistance Act and under existing country-to-country memorandums of agreement.

(e) APS are positioned and contain categories of stocks as follows: APS-1 (CONUS)—OPROJ stocks, sustainment stocks, and ammunition; APS-3 (Afloat) – pre-positioned sets, ammunition, OPROJ stocks, and sustainment stocks; APS-4 (Pacific and Northeast Asia) – pre-positioned sets, OPROJ stocks, sustainment stocks, ammunition, and watercraft; APS-5 (Southwest Asia)—pre-positioned stocks, OPROJ stocks, sustainment stocks, ammunition, and watercraft.

(6) **US Marine Corps.** The Marine Corps depends heavily on afloat pre-positioning, known as the maritime pre-positioning force (MPF). MPF is a strategic deployment option that quickly combines the substantial PREPO equipment and supplies loaded aboard ships of an MPS squadron with a Marine air-ground task force (MAGTF) to establish a formidable combined arms force capable of sustained operations. The MAGTF and Navy support element (NSE) personnel, selected equipment, and combat aircraft are flown into the objective area where the MPS operations occur. The MPS are specifically constructed or modified RO/RO and lift-on/lift-off ships that are forward deployed in two self-contained squadrons. Each squadron carries the unit equipment and 30 days of supplies for one brigade-size MAGTF. Additionally, each ship is outfitted with NSE equipment consisting of the camp support and lighterage needed to discharge cargo over unimproved ports or over the beach. Each ship carries a cross load of unit equipment, supplies, POL, and potable water; thereby eliminating the need to discharge all vessels in order to obtain required types and quantities of equipment and cargo. However, the LMSRs in the MPF are

> **During Operations DESERT SHIELD and DESERT STORM, afloat pre-positioning ships sailed from forward bases in Diego Garcia to the Middle East. The war reserve cargo on board these ships included subsistence, general supplies and equipment, packaged fuel, construction and barrier materials, ammunition, and medical supplies. One semi-submersible heavy lift vessel carried port operating equipment (e.g., tugboats, floating cranes, utility landing craft, rough terrain forklifts, containers, and support parts). These ships proved indispensable during the operation's first days, providing a readily available source of supplies and the capability to begin water terminal operations immediately upon the arrival of follow-on sealift.**
>
> **SOURCE: Final Report to Congress**
> **Conduct of the Persian Gulf War, April 1992**

not capable of providing POL over the shore as the legacy MPF vessels are equipped to provide. There are two MPS squadrons, with MPS Squadron 2 positioned in the Indian Ocean (Diego Garcia) and MPS Squadron 3 positioned in the Western Pacific (Guam and Saipan). MPS cargo may be discharged pier side in three days or "in stream" in five days by NSE personnel composed of naval beach group and cargo handling battalion personnel, as well as Marine Corps personnel airlifted to the objective area. The Marine Corps also maintains land-based PREPO assets in Norway sufficient to support a Marine expeditionary brigade with equipment and supplies.

(7) **US Air Force.** The Air Force pre-positions equipment and supplies both afloat and on land. The current Air Force pre-positioned fleet consists of two ammunition carrying vessels under MPS OPCON. On land, the Air Force pre-positions standard air munitions packages, theater ammunition stocks, and life support and flightline support complexes. A unique capability also pre-positioned by the Air Force is the bare base life support system intended for use in contingencies. The Basic Expeditionary Airfield Resources (BEAR) systems and equipment provide vital equipment and supplies necessary to beddown and support combat forces at expeditionary sites with limited infrastructure and support facilities. BEAR systems and equipment are aggregated into unit type code "sets" or "packages" and are designed to be scalable and air transportable. BEAR sets include the Swift BEAR 150 Personnel Housekeeping Set, the BEAR 550 Initial Housekeeping Set, 550 Follow-On Housekeeping Set, the Industrial Operations Set, the Initial Flightline Set, and the Follow-On Flightline Set. BEAR sets also include legacy sets such as Harvest Eagle and Harvest Falcon, but these sets are being phased out as the BEAR sets arrive. As a minimum, each deployment location must have a runway and parking ramp suitable for aircraft operations and a source of water that can be made potable.

(8) **US Navy.** Incorporated in both MPS Squadron 2 and MPS Squadron 3 will be one dry cargo/ammunition replenishment ship that provides a wide range of supplies and stocks to the Navy and Marine Corps expeditionary forces. These ships carry dry cargo, ammunition, and fuel and are capable of operating with Navy carrier strike groups and amphibious ready groups at sea. In addition, two aviation support vessels are maintained in ROS-5 readiness for the Marine Corps; one each is stationed on the East and the West Coasts of the US.

PRE-POSITIONING SUPPORT IN KOSOVO

...Other logistics successes included timely intertheater movement of stocks of preferred munitions, including pre-positioned munitions ships, and effective and efficient management of theater fuel distribution, including the use of pre-positioned ships.

SOURCE: Defense Secretary William S. Cohen and General Hugh Shelton, Joint Statement on the Kosovo After Action Review, October 1999

b. **Forward Stocking.** DLA's OCONUS distribution depots are located in Germany, Italy, Kuwait, Korea, Japan, Guam, and Hawaii. These depots offer opportunities to forward position stock of OCONUS customers and enhance the theater distribution system by forward stocking high usage items closer to the operational area, thereby enabling parts and supplies to be distributed in a timely manner. DLA distribution center depots in Southwest Asia, Germany, and Korea also have theater consolidation and shipping point capabilities.

8. **Intermodal Systems**

a. Intermodal refers to the transferring of passengers or transshipping of cargo among two or more modes of transportation. In concert with intermodal distribution, containerization facilitates and optimizes carrying of cargo via multiple modes of transport (highway, rail, sea, inland waterway, and air) without intermediate handling of the contents. Intermodalism and the use of the DOD intermodal container system are integral to the efficiency and effectiveness of DTS support to joint operations. The term "DOD intermodal container system" refers to all DOD-owned, -leased, or -controlled intermodal containers and flatracks as well as supporting equipment such as generator sets, chassis, CHE, MHE, portable ramps, information systems, and other infrastructure that supports DTS. Containerships can improve closure of selected combat support and combat service support forces, provide massive sustainment cargo delivery capability, and can be used as an alternate means to transport unit equipment (particularly for combat support and combat service support forces) when adequate RO/RO vessels are not available. Recognizing this, the DOD goal is to maximize the use of these assets and the vast commercial intermodal capability that is available on a day-to-day basis.

b. Decreased handling results in reduced delivery times, less damage to cargo, and enhances shipment integrity by reducing chances of a split shipment.

c. During deliberate and crisis action planning, unit equipment, sustainment, and resupply (including ammunition) cargo suitable for containerization should be identified and appropriately coded consistent with in-theater infrastructure capabilities and the CCDR's CONOPS.

d. SDDC provides global intermodal equipment and services to DOD and other USG departments and agencies. It is responsible for managing the DOD's containerized ammunition distribution system as well as leased intermodal equipment. It provides such items as 20- and 40-foot International Organization for Standardization containers, ammunition grade containers, flatracks, food and fuel grade tanks, and other types of containers and intermodal equipment. Through the use of SDDC's global intermodal contracts, DOD has worldwide intermodal capabilities that allow SDDC to acquire thousands of pieces of intermodal equipment, including chassis or line haul assets essential to move equipment forward.

For details on the types of intermodal assets and procedures for their use, refer to JP 4-09, Distribution Operations.

CHAPTER IV
EMPLOYMENT OF THE DEFENSE TRANSPORTATION SYSTEM

> *"The art of war is simple enough. Find out where your enemy is. Get at him as soon as you can. Strike him as hard as you can, and keep moving on."*
>
> **Ulysses S. Grant, statement to John Hill Brinton, at the start of his Tennessee River Campaign, early 1862, as quoted in Personal Memoirs of John H. Brinton, Major and Surgeon USV [United States Volunteers], 1861–1865 (1914) by John Hill Brinton**

1. Purpose

This chapter describes the procedures used to forecast movement requirements, allocate resources, execute movement of people and cargo, and report on those movements. It further discusses employment of military movement resources during CONUS civil transportation disruptions. It is important to realize that these processes are interactive, especially with regard to crisis and wartime procedures. The normal sequence of events is requirements determination, allocation of resources, execution, and reporting. Refer to Appendix A, "Transportation Priorities," for movement priorities.

2. Requirements Determination and Submission

a. General

(1) CJCS's roles and functions include assisting the President and SecDef in providing for the strategic direction of the Armed Forces of the United States; responsibility for strategic and contingency planning; advising SecDef on requirements, programs, and budget; and assisting the President and SecDef in performing their command functions. To these ends, CJCS oversees the activities of the CCMDs. CJCS's Joint Logistics Operations Center (JLOC) or JTB, if activated, allows him to maintain cognizance over transportation requirements and capabilities as well as ensure that information is available for determining and adjusting allocations of common-user resources and priorities during wartime or contingencies.

(2) Movement requirements are established by competent authority within the Joint Staff, the Military Departments, CCMDs, other DOD and USG departments and agencies, and the Executive Branch of the government.

(3) DOD movement requirements may be fulfilled using one or more modes of transportation. Shipments are documented in accordance with the *DTR*.

b. Deployment and Distribution Operations (DDOC) Fusion Center

(1) The DDOC Fusion Center is the C2 structure used by USTRANSCOM to exercise C2 of DTS and is grounded in the principle of centralized control of DTS and the decentralized execution of qualified movement requirements. The structure is made up of the C2 elements at USTRANSCOM to include TCCs and other specialized transportation

organizations. This structure is used to orchestrate and optimize DTS operations in support of CCDRs and other DOD customers. Joint members of the structure are linked by C2 and communications systems and optimize available strategic lift against DTS requirements. Figure IV-1 depicts the DDOC Fusion Center structure.

(2) The Fusion Center has seven key elements with numerous additional liaison officers and divisions to support global operations.

(a) USTRANSCOM DDOC. Focal point for DTS operations.

(b) 618 Air Operations Center (Tanker Airlift Control Center) (AOC) (TACC). Plans, schedules, tasks, and controls intertheater and common-user airlift.

(c) SDDC Command Operations Center. Plans, schedules, and manages resources to satisfy movement requirements using common-user surface lift.

(d) MSC Command Information Center. In conjunction with MSC program managers, plans, schedules, manages, and operates ships to support DOD sealift requirements.

(e) Global Patient Movement Integration Center. Resources theater patient movement requirements centers globally to plan, schedule, and validate patient movement (PM) requests and regulate PM.

(f) Joint Operational Support Airlift Center. Plans and schedules a CONUS-based operational support aircraft pool provided by the Services.

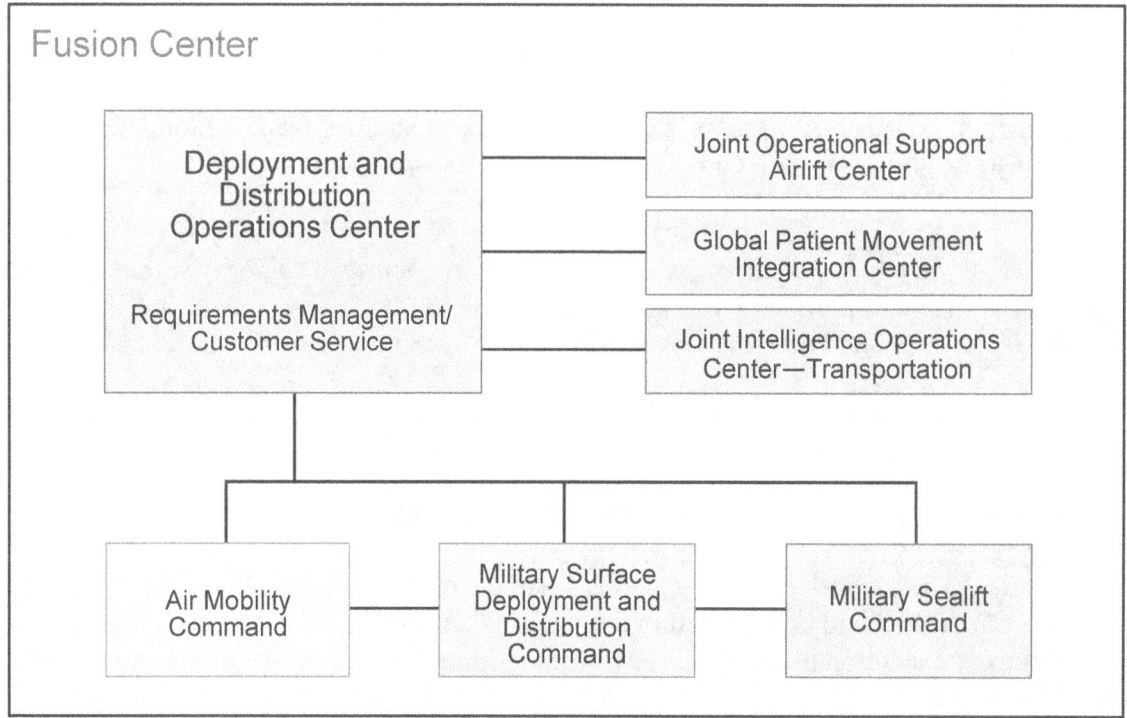

Figure IV-1. Fusion Center

(g) Joint Intelligence Operations Center—Transportation. Provides OCONUS destination intelligence support to the Fusion Center.

c. **Theater-Joint Transportation Board.** The role of the T-JTB is to resolve contentious transportation issues within the command at the operational level, such as allocating transportation assets apportioned to the theater among components for unit movement and non-unit movement.

d. **Peacetime Movement Requirements**

(1) The Services and DLA are responsible for the determination, collection, and submission of the movement requirements.

(2) Peacetime movement requirement forecasts are normally submitted for each mode in the categories shown in Figure IV-2.

(3) Forecasts become operational upon the actual offering of the movement requirement to the TCC by the user or shipper.

(4) Movement requirements, planning factors, and methodology need periodic reevaluation by the Services and other agencies to ensure reasonableness and accuracy.

(5) Non-DOD agencies will submit their movement requirements for DOD common-user transportation to the Deputy Assistant Under Secretary of Defense (Transportation Policy) for approval. The sponsoring agency must certify that the movement is in the national interest, commercial services are unavailable or unsuitable, and reimbursement will be provided to DOD for services rendered.

e. **CJCS-Sponsored and CCDR-Sponsored Exercises**

(1) General

(a) CJCS requires annual submission and updating of all CJCS Exercise

---

Peacetime Movement Requirement Categories

Airlift Requirements
1. Channel airlift
2. Special assignment airlift mission
3. Joint airborne and air transportability training
4. Exercises
5. Commercial door to door service
6. Aeromedical evacuation

Sealift Requirements
1. Intertheater (including continental United States [CONUS]-originated shipments)
2. Intratheater
3. Coastal movements
4. Exercises

CONUS Civil Transportation Requirements
1. Rail traffic
2. Motor traffic
3. Inland waterway traffic
4. Commercial express service

Figure IV-2. Peacetime Movement Requirement Categories

Program proposals by CCDRs for the next 5 fiscal years. Proposals serve as planning documents for resourcing future exercise funding, transportation, and force requirements.

(b) When approved, the Joint Staff publishes the 5-year schedule of CJCS-sponsored and CCDR-sponsored exercises as the joint training master schedule (JTMS).

(2) **Responsibility.** CCDRs are responsible for revising exercise requirements as necessary and for submitting exercise updates to the JTMS as required.

f. **Wartime and Contingency Movement Requirements**

(1) **General.** The supported CCDR, in coordination with supporting commanders and Services, establishes movement requirements. This is accomplished by developing a deployment and/or redeployment TPFDD in JOPES. The TPFDD can be developed from an existing or modified TPFDD, or a totally new TPFDD can be built in a no-plan situation. The supporting and supported commanders, and their components, review this TPFDD, source the various requirements, and then refine or establish a detailed transportation timeline. When completed, USTRANSCOM and supported CCDRs validate requirements in JOPES for the appropriate TCC to plan, schedule, and execute movement.

(2) **Planned Crises/War Lift Requirements.** There are two categories of requirements: forces that support the deployment and redeployment of units and their equipment, and those that sustain the force. Additionally, other CCDRs have day-to-day operating requirements for the forces in-place in their theaters. Supported CCDR requirements are formulated during planning and include the time phasing for deploying units and supporting materiel. The latter includes requirements to sustain pre-positioned and deploying forces.

(a) **Deployment Lift Requirements.** The supported CCDR is allocated forces and other resources to meet the assigned mission. The CCDR's force flow for requirements is developed by the supported CCDR's components, the supporting CCDRs, the Services, and other DOD agencies as appropriate. Sourced, refined, and validated deployment requirements in JOPES will be reviewed incrementally by appropriate commanders via the GCCS. When validated, USTRANSCOM retrieves updated movement requirements from JOPES and schedules transportation assets to move against them. The schedules are available in JOPES and its subsystem Web Scheduling and Movement for visibility by the joint planning and execution community (JPEC).

(b) **Sustainment Movement**

1. **Channels.** Priority sustainment requirements move on predetermined channels validated by the Services or supported CCDR, as appropriate, and USTRANSCOM. The supported GCC will sub-allocate the theater sustainment lift (including mail) to their components. In order to optimize theater sustainment lift, the supported GCC may establish a JDDOC. This should be done in the initial stages of operation order and TPFDD execution. With representation from all theater Service components, the JDDOC receives advance notification of incoming forces and cargo and makes modal decisions regarding the onward movement of the cargo. Through the use of the

JDDOC, the supported GCC provides deployed forces with a focal point to address prioritization issues. Additionally the JDDOC can make decisions that support time-definite delivery and can result in significant cost savings for the supported customer. This should be done in the initial stages of TPFDD execution. When USTRANSCOM is unable to deconflict competing CCDRs' demands, CJCS will convene the CJCS JTB to allocate lift in accordance with its charter (see Appendix B, "Charter of the Chairman of the Joint Chiefs of Staff Joint Transportation Board"). Requirements may be generated by component commands as authorized by the respective supported CCDRs.

2. **Worldwide Express.** WWX provides international commercial express package (letter to 300 pounds) time-definite, door-to-door pickup and delivery, with accurate ITV. Under the WWX concept, wartime or contingency operations critical cargo with definite delivery times will be picked up by express carriers at depots, installations, or ports of embarkation (POEs) and moved via their commercial routes structure for delivery to the AOR. The vast majority of airlift sustainment will move on established channel missions (includes already established express services). However, when other options are exhausted during a contingency, USTRANSCOM is prepared to establish an additional express service (channel contingency mission) to move mission-critical items rapidly to the supported AOR at the request of the supported CCDR. Of equal importance is the return movement of critical reparable assets to the depot or source of repair for subsequent resupply. This express service could be activated by USTRANSCOM either concurrently with execution of a CCDR's operation or at the request of the supported CCDR. The CCDR should consider express service implementation no later than C+3 day to ensure critical sustainment for combat forces engaged in initial combat operations. The required frequency and destinations for this service should also be determined at this point. When requirements exceed capability, the supported CCDR allocates capability among the Services. Services should forecast and prioritize movement requirements for critical classes of supply and assets that have an immediate impact on combat capability to USTRANSCOM for execution. All requirements will be validated by the supported CCDR to USTRANSCOM and moved on predetermined channels.

(3) **Theater Distribution.** Distribution is the process of synchronizing all elements of the logistic system to deliver the right things to the right place at the right time to support the CCDR. The distribution system is a complex network tailored to meet the requirements of the military force across the range of military operations. This network may be overlaid on existing HN infrastructure that must be shared with the HN and often with other military, civilian, and multinational forces participating in the same operation. Combinations of US military, DOD civilian, HN, multinational, and contractor organizations operate the nodes

NOTE: Hazardous materials (HAZMAT) are not covered under the basic service of worldwide express (WWX). HAZMAT under WWX is allowed based on what the carrier is authorized to move for its commercial customers. The customer will be charged the accessorial fee for that service. Please contact the carriers' HAZMAT telephone numbers listed in the WWX web page: https://private.amc.af.mil/A4/wwx/.

Per WWX Website

and modes of transportation that distribute the forces and sustainment assets. These organizations collect and report data to a network of HQ responsible for processing the data into information and issuing instructions to the node and mode operators. Figure IV-3 depicts principles of theater distribution.

For more information on distribution, see JP 4-09, Distribution Operations.

(4) **Time-Sensitive Lift Requirements.** Short notice transportation requirements due to changing tactical situations or other developments may require a rapid response by airlift movement. Unplanned requirements are categorized as CCDR lift requirements to support operation execution. As part of their air apportionment decisions, JFCs should consider the apportioning of aviation assets to supported or subordinate commanders for time-sensitive lift requirements.

(a) **Patient Movement.** Intertheater PM is supported by USTRANSCOM air mobility resources. Intertheater PM operations serve as the global interface between the theater and CONUS PM and is validated by USTRANSCOM Command Surgeon's Office as the single manager for implementation of policy and standardization of global PM; C2 is maintained by the 618 AOC (TACC) to carry out the PM. The transferring medical treatment facility (MTF) is responsible for the transportation of patients between the MTF and the designated staging facility or to the aircraft. AMC will use preplanned, opportune, or retrograde aircraft missions to pick up patients from staging facilities at designated theater PM interface airfields. AMC maintains C2 over intertheater air mobility and supporting non-theater assigned elements.

For more information on patient movement, see JP 4-02, Health Service Support.

(b) **Pre-Execution**

1. Special assignment airlift missions (SAAMs) can be used for airlift requirements (such as pre-positioning) prior to or during TPFDD execution. Procedures governing their use are contained in appropriate publications, such as the *DTR.* During a developing crisis and before movement begins, Services or other airlift coordination agencies should transmit SAAM requests supporting the pending operation directly to the supported

---

Principles of Theater Distribution

- Centralized management
- Optimize the distribution system
- Velocity over mass
- Maximize throughput
- Reduce customer wait time

- Minimize stockpiling
- Continuous, seamless, two-way flow of resources
- Time definite delivery

Figure IV-3. Principles of Theater Distribution

Short-notice transportation requirements may require a rapid response by airlift movement.

CCDR for approval, or as directed by supporting or supported CCDRs. Information copies are provided to USTRANSCOM and other concerned agencies. The supported CCDR may validate the request to the USTRANSCOM DDOC Fusion Center.

2. USTRANSCOM allocates the air mobility assets to support the force deployment(s) and identifies air mobility assets available to AMC, which support all other worldwide requirements.

(c) **Execution**

1. During a deployment, unexpected time-sensitive movement requirements may occur. USTRANSCOM may support these requirements, by airlift, in one of three ways:

a. AMC-operated or commercially contracted civilian aircraft,

b. Request for an airlift reallocation from the CJCS JTB, or

c. Use of assets temporarily available through agreements with allies, such as the NATO Civil Aviation Agency, or foreign airline resources.

2. Urgent requirements are identified by supported CCDRs to the supporting CCDRs or Services and USTRANSCOM, with information to AMC and CJCS JTB. USTRANSCOM and AMC determine the most feasible air transportation solution available and schedule the requirement(s). If assets are not readily available, AMC informs USTRANSCOM, which informs the supported CCDR. The supported CCDR decides

whether to defer movement of a lower priority requirement or, as a last resort, requests reallocation of air mobility from the CJCS JTB. The requirements and scheduled lift will be entered into the JOPES and JOPES subsystem Web Simulation and Modeling deployment database as expeditiously as possible. An option always remains to divert cargo of lower priority to sealift.

(d) **Air Mobility Division (AMD).** The AMD is made up of an air mobility control team, airlift control team, air refueling control team, and aeromedical evacuation control team. The AMD will integrate and direct the execution of theater assigned or attached Service organic mobility forces operating in the AOR or joint operations area in support of JFC objectives. OPCON of USTRANSCOM assigned air mobility forces supporting, but not attached to, the JTF or subordinate command will remain with AMC. This expansion of C2 systems requires the AMD to interface with the 618 AOC (TACC), other AMDs if required, and the joint air operations center (if established) combat operations and combat plans divisions to ensure air mobility missions are included in the air tasking order.

For further information on AMD, see JP 3-17, Air Mobility Operations.

3. Planning and Allocation of Resources

a. **Peacetime.** See Figure IV-4.

(1) **Air Mobility.** Upon receiving air mobility requirements from USTRANSCOM, AMC and the geographic CCMDs possessing theater-assigned airlift assets plan how to best use available capability (including commercial contract) to meet those requirements. If air mobility resources appear insufficient to meet requirements, AMC and supported CCDRs identify possible shortages of tonnage and/or space by geographic area before making an initial space assignment and advising shipping agencies. If agreement cannot be reached among the shipping services and AMC, the problem will be referred to USTRANSCOM for resolution. Problems not resolved by USTRANSCOM will be raised to the CJCS JLOC or JTB, if activated, for resolution.

(2) **Sealift.** Upon receipt of sealift requirements, MSC plans its fleet operations. Cargo requirements that exceed the MSC-controlled fleet may be met through charters. If sealift resources are still insufficient to meet emergency or contingency requirements, provisions exist for activation of organic government-owned sealift (FSSs, LMSR ships, and the MARAD RRF). If sealift resources are still insufficient, additional shipping can be acquired through a variety of access programs to commercial shipping.

(3) **CONUS Surface Transportation and Ports.** Upon receipt of military movement requirements, SDDC (as the SPM) assigns the workload to military ocean terminals and commercial port facilities. In addition, SDDC may arrange for the intra-CONUS movement of DOD cargo by commercial highway and rail carriers and notifies USTRANSCOM of any shortfalls in terminal or intra-CONUS transportation capabilities that it cannot resolve. Shortfalls that cannot be resolved by USTRANSCOM will be referred to the CJCS JLOC or JTB, if activated.

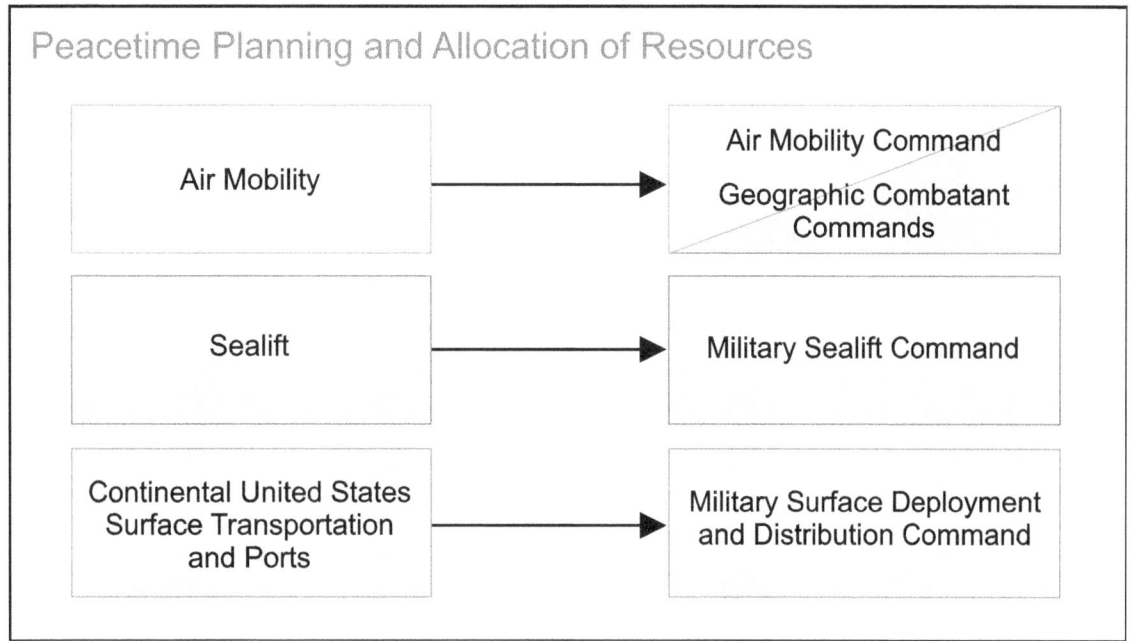

Figure IV-4. Peacetime Planning and Allocation of Resources

b. **Wartime or Contingency**

(1) CJCSI 3110.01, *Joint Strategic Capabilities Plan (JSCP),* and GEF, are two of many planning directives available to the CCDRs. SecDef and CJCS, through these planning directives, task CCDRs to develop plans (OPLANs) for specific contingencies based on current military capabilities. The documents provide planning guidance to the Services for the support of the CCDRs in execution of assigned tasks. CJCSI 3110.11, *Mobility Supplement to Joint Strategic Capabilities Plan*, identifies common-user lift resources used for the transportation feasibility analysis of plans.

(2) The supported CCDR develops a CONOPS based upon guidance in CJCSI 3110.01, *Joint Strategic Capabilities Plan and the GEF.* Subordinate component commanders are then tasked to determine specific forces (unit) and supply (non-unit) requirements (including personnel replacements) and the recommended time phasing of these requirements. The component commands' force and support requirements are submitted to the supported CCDR, who integrates them with any other requirements to develop the TPFDD. The strategic movement of these requirements is then analyzed against the specified transportation assets found in CJCSI 3110.11, *Mobility Supplement to Joint Strategic Capabilities Plan*, using the Joint Flow and Analysis System for Transportation in order to determine gross transportation feasibility of the plan. Refinements are made as required to the total movement, and TCCs prepare movement tables for the entire TPFDD in order to gauge deployment capability. USTRANSCOM assesses feasibility of the complete TPFDD in accordance with the joint combat capability assessment process so it will be ready for immediate execution. Supporting commanders are to ensure that their specific forces are identified, accurately portrayed (e.g., number of passengers and actual Level 4 cargo detail), and available to meet deployment schedules.

4. Execution

a. **Peacetime.** TCCs apply capability to move requirements in accordance with their planning and within the guidelines of the priority system. (See Appendix A, "Transportation Priorities.") Problems not resolved at the USTRANSCOM and/or Service level will be raised to the CJCS JLOC or JTB, if activated, for resolution.

b. **Contingency and Wartime**

(1) Upon receipt of a warning order, alert order, or other indication of a potential deployment, USTRANSCOM establishes communications with the J-4, the supported and supporting CCDRs, the Services, and TCCs (see Figure IV-5). USTRANSCOM begins an immediate review of deployment plans and TPFDD to ensure their applicability and assists the supported CCDR in updating the TPFDD. When no TPFDD exists for an operation, the JPEC creates a TPFDD in JOPES. CJCSM 3122 Series, *Joint Operation Planning and Execution System (JOPES),* and CJCSM 3130 Series, *Adaptive Planning and Execution (APEX),* addresses joint operation planning, policies, procedures, and TPFDD development and deployment execution. As the situation develops, USTRANSCOM, in coordination with the TCCs, develops estimates of the feasibility to support various deployment options and provides comments and recommendations to the supported CCDR and the CJCS JLOC or JTB, if activated. USTRANSCOM personnel monitor port, transportation, and lines of communications capabilities and limitations to determine their impact on the deployment. If needed, cargo diversion teams, comprised of supported CCDR, USTRANSCOM, and Service representatives, should be used at SPOEs and APOEs to preclude saturation of the sealift and airlift systems.

(2) When implementation of multiple plans is contemplated, USTRANSCOM obtains deployment priorities from CJCS during the Global Force Management Board and advises the rest of the deployment community. USTRANSCOM provides supported commanders, the CJCS JLOC and JTB, when activated, with the impact of these priorities on closure times, transportation, and ongoing operations.

Defense Transportation System Contingency and Wartime Execution

United States Transportation Command:

- Establishes communications.
- Reviews force deployment and sustainment plans.
- Develops feasibility estimates.
- Monitors port, transportation, and lines of communications.
- Develops strategic airlift and sealift schedules.

Figure IV-5. Defense Transportation System Contingency and Wartime Execution

(3) In a no-plan situation, or when real world crisis situations change the resource apportionment planned in CJCSI 3110.11, *Mobility Supplement to Joint Strategic Capabilities Plan*, USTRANSCOM reassigns strategic lift capabilities to the CCDRs based upon the urgency of the situation and informs CJCS JLOC and JTB, if activated. As the situation changes, USTRANSCOM reviews the allocation and recommends appropriate changes. If USTRANSCOM is unable to allocate lift to the satisfaction of competing CCDRs, CJCS, through the JTB, adjudicates the allocations.

(4) Once capability is allocated to the CCDRs' requirements, each CCDR's T-JTB or equivalent activity must immediately prioritize and allocate that theater's capability among competing lift requirements. The supported CCDR communicates the deployment and resupply decisions to USTRANSCOM for execution and informs the CJCS JLOC or JTB, if activated. Other CCDRs validate frequency channel requirements and allocate appropriate lift capability to their requirements.

(5) Services are proportionally assigned strategic lift resources for their resupply and personnel replacements based upon supported CCDR allocation in the JOPES database. Shipper Service HQs and DLA provide advocates to assist the commanders with prioritization of lift at CONUS ports.

(6) USTRANSCOM coordinates the execution of CJCS and CCDR lift allocation decisions for transportation resources that support the plans being executed. As the DOD single manager for transportation (other than Service organic or theater-assigned assets) CDRUSTRANSCOM:

(a) Directs the implementation of CJCS and CCDR lift decisions to the TCCs, force providers, and Service materiel and personnel managers.

(b) Apportions lift capabilities for resupply and personnel replacements or fillers among the Services in accordance with the guidance of the supported CCDR(s).

(c) Adjusts movement plans, schedules, and modes of transport.

(7) For supported CCDR lift requirements outside the GCC's AOR, USTRANSCOM applies lift resources according to GCC allocation decisions as expressed by the GCC.

(8) USTRANSCOM monitors and provides lift status on deploying military forces, replacement personnel and sustainment to the Joint Staff, supported and supporting commanders, and the Services.

(9) USTRANSCOM, through SDDC, provides a port management cell and/or reinforcement of existing cells to the supported joint task force(s) and/or CCDR(s). SDDC will assist with OPLAN development and analysis, conduct assessment of ports, and recommend the size and type of port operations required. The cell will establish liaison with HN port authorities and develop statements of work for contracting facilities and stevedore labor, if available. The cell will provide automated data processing and communications

capabilities in support of water terminal operations. It will provide common-user container management services and prioritize the port operator's workload based on the GCC's intent.

(10) USTRANSCOM attempts to resolve transportation conflicts during deployment and refers unresolved issues to the CJCS JLOC or JTB, if activated, for action.

5. In-Transit Visibility Reporting

a. **Integrated Data Environment/Global Transportation Network Convergence (IGC).** IGC is a single system that integrates information from a variety of DTS automated information systems to provide ITV and C2 data support. IGC supports the President, SecDef, the CCDRs, the Services, and other DOD customers with information to better manage their warfighting and logistic capabilities. IGC is the ITV system of record providing expanded common integrated data and application services enabling distribution solutions. IGC enables a common logistics picture, distribution visibility, and material asset/ITV.

b. ITV is the ability to track the identity, status, and location of DOD units, non-unit cargo (excluding bulk POL), passengers, patients, and personal property from origin to consignee or destination across the range of military operations. ITV of assets moving through DTS or in support of DOD operations is an essential element of the DOD warfighting capability and is required by the supported CCDRs. The transportation tracking number (TTN) and transportation control number (TCN) are alphanumeric character sets assigned to a shipment (unit move and sustainment) to maintain ITV. IGC links the TCN to the military standard requisitioning and issue procedure (MILSTRIP) number, if available, and to commercial express carrier tracking numbers, if applicable. The Defense Logistics Management System (DLMS) establishes a baseline set of data necessary to support information exchange technology, such as manifests, electronic data interchange (EDI), and automated identification technology (AIT) devices. Service-specific logistics systems apply DLMS standards to enable movement data which is consolidated in IGC. Users can query various ITV data relevant to their cargo in IGC. IGC also provides cargo detail to various common operational pictures, such as the Single Mobility System, the Battled Command Support and Sustainment System, and others. The TTN will link ITV data to JOPES in support of OPLAN execution. This gives the user multiple ways to track forces, equipment, and items. See the *Defense Transportation Regulation* for specific information governing the use of TTNs and TCNs.

c. While USTRANSCOM is the designated DOD proponent for the development of a comprehensive, integrated DOD ITV capability, it does not execute ITV independently. The ITV process consists of numerous players who must follow designated business procedures to provide accurate source data, prompt nodal updates, shipment status information, and shipment receipt notices. The use of AIT facilitates improved data accuracy and collection processes raising confidence in ITV information shared among various automated information systems. Key ITV players include, but are not limited to, deploying units, node and port operators, commercial transportation service providers, installations, and depots. Each plays a critical role in ensuring seamless ITV by providing movement information (manifest transmission) to IGC and Web Simulation and Modeling within the following ITV timeliness criteria outlined by the DTR, 4500.9-R.

(1) Ocean shipments.

(a) Commercial liner and charter service: within 12 hours of the event (goal of 4 hours).

(b) Exercise and wartime unit and sustainment moves on US Navy ships: within 24 hours of the event (goal of 4 hours).

(2) All intratheater cargo and passenger movements (all modes): within 2 hours of the event.

(3) All air, truck, and rail cargo and passenger intertheater movements: within 1 hour of the event.

d. **Unit Cargo.** Unit cargo includes all unit equipment, accompanying supplies, Service pre-positioned forces and afloat pre-positioned equipment, and war reserve stocks. IGC receives unit movement data from various systems from point of origin, through a POE and port of debarkation (POD), and within the CONUS and theater. Generation of *Defense Transportation Regulation* compliant deployment data is a unit responsibility. Global Air Transportation Execution System (GATES) is the primary POE and POD systems for sealift and air mobility, respectively. Cargo Movement Operations System (CMOS) is the primary system at US Air Force non-AMC-owned organizations. Where GATES/CMOS capability is not readily available, alternative unit data capture solutions are coordinated by the lift provider and the moving organization and tailored to meet ITV requirements. AIT protocols should also be employed as appropriate anywhere along the movement pipeline to provide timelier, accurate movement updates.

e. **Non-Unit-Related Cargo.** Non-unit related cargo includes all equipment and supplies requiring transportation to an operational area, other than those identified as the equipment or accompanying supplies of a specific unit (e.g., resupply, military support for allies, and support for nonmilitary programs such as civil relief). IGC receives source shipment information from DOD and commercial vendor shippers, nodal updates from key DOD and commercial logistic activities (consolidation points, aerial ports and seaports, theater onward movement locations, etc.), and shipment status information from commercial carriers. The origin shipping activity is responsible for generating the appropriate movement documentation. IGC receives DTR-compliant source shipment information from the Distribution Standard System for DLA shipments. As shipments arrive and depart from seaports and aerial ports, IGC receives updates from GATES/CMOS. Finally, IGC receives shipment status information from commercial carriers and vendors using industry EDI standards. AIT protocols are also employed as appropriate to facilitate timely, accurate data capture.

f. **Unit Personnel.** Unit-move personnel include all civilian and military passengers directly attached to, and moving with, a deploying unit. IGC receives unit passenger data from source systems, POE and POD systems, and CONUS and theater consignee transportation systems. Generation of DTR-compliant deployment data is a unit responsibility. As passengers move through AMC aerial ports, GATES updates the manifest information in IGC and offers inbound passenger manifest data to the APOD and other receiving activities for planning and JRSOI management activities. Upon passengers' arrival at the APOD, information about their onward movement will be passed to IGC. Where there is not a GATES capability readily available, alternative unit data capture solutions are coordinated by the lift provider and the moving organizations and tailored to meet ITV requirements. The use of the common access card is directed by the Deputy Secretary of Defense and will meet enhanced data accuracy while expediting passenger manifesting and processing procedures.

g. **Non-Unit-Related Personnel.** Non-unit related personnel (NURP) include all personnel requiring transportation to or from an operational area, other than those assigned to a specific unit (e.g., filler personnel; replacements; temporary duty or temporary additional duty personnel; civilians; medical evacuees; and retrograde personnel). GATES serves as the primary information collection point for reservations and booking of NURP. The originating installation transportation office electronically requests airlift through GATES, which in turn provides both schedules and seat confirmation to the requester. GATES also prepares passenger manifests for departing aircraft and transmits that information to IGC. For non-unit personnel traveling from other than GATES-supported locations, passenger manifesting is accomplished and forwarded to IGC. DOD does not track passengers moving on scheduled commercial transportation as a robust commercial capability currently exists.

h. **Lift Assets.** An equally critical aspect of ITV is visibility over airlift, sealift, and surface lift assets (aircraft, ships, and road and rail conveyances). Visibility of lift assets in-transit or scheduled for movement is key to the C2 of those assets, port management, and scheduling the movement of both unit and non-unit cargo and personnel. USTRANSCOM port software programs feed status of shipments to IGC, Services, and DLA software programs. AMC schedules and manages the execution of organic and AMC chartered strategic airlift through the Global Decision Support System (GDSS). The GDSS passes airlift schedules and arrival and departure information to the IGC. Similarly, MSC provides sealift schedules and updates for organic and chartered lift assets to IGC via the MSC integrated command, control, and communication system, while commercial carriers pass arrival and departure event information via EDI. There is no single DOD system for tracking all road and rail schedules; however, there are some DOD automated information systems and AITs that monitor portions of road and rail moves. These modes are critical to the movement of DOD assets because nearly 90 percent of DTS surface lift is provided by commercial carriers.

6. Layering of Automated Identification Technology to Promote Asset and In-Transit Visibility

a. **Automated Identification Technology.** AIT is a suite of technologies enabling the automatic capture of data, thereby enhancing the ability to identify, track, document, and control materiel, deploying and redeploying forces, equipment, personnel, and sustainment cargo. AIT encompasses a variety of data storage or carrier technologies, such as bar codes, magnetic strips, integrated circuit cards, optical laser discs (optical memory cards or compact discs), satellite tracking, and radio frequency identification (RFID) tags used for marking or "tagging" individual items, equipment, air pallets, or containers. The consistent application of AIT in the distribution and supply chain processes throughout DOD is key to deriving the most asset visibility and ITV in the DOD enterprise.

b. The Under Secretary of Defense for Acquisition, Technology and Logistics designated USTRANSCOM, in its role as the DPO, as the lead functional proponent for RFID and related AIT implementation throughout the DOD supply chain. A key goal of USTRANSCOM in this functional proponency is to ensure that AIT use throughout the supply chain is coordinated to maximize its effectiveness, with minimal redundancies or conflicting technologies, as a means to achieve asset visibility. In executing this responsibility, USTRANSCOM facilitated the development of standard applications of AIT in the DOD supply chain (see Figure IV-6). While these designations of specific AIT are significant, USTRANSCOM is constantly working with the Services, DOD and the CCDRs to refine and adjust these requirements as technology breakthroughs and business processes dictate change.

7. Employment of Military Movement Resources During a Disruption of Civil Transportation in the Continental United States

a. **Background.** If CONUS civil transportation service is disrupted and SecDef so directs, the military-owned capability specified in this section can be applied within CONUS to help meet military movement requirements. The Services, CCDRs, DLA, SDDC, and AMC are responsible for providing data or making available vehicles and aircraft with associated operations, maintenance, and administration.

b. **Authorization.** Upon the recommendation of CDRUSTRANSCOM, CJCS may recommend to SecDef authorization of the use of military vehicles or military aircraft to augment the civil transportation capability during disruption.

8. Non-Department of Defense Shipments

Background. Allies and international organizations with which DOD has an ACSA or similar agreement may submit requests for transportation in accordance with those agreements and DOD implementing regulations. Other non-DOD entities, including other USG departments and agencies, commercial or private entities, intergovernmental organizations, nongovernmental organizations, and commercial agencies requesting cargo, passenger and/or human remains movement via DTS submit their cargo movement requirements for an exception to policy to Assistant Deputy Under Secretary of Defense (Transportation Policy) for approval unless DOD directives or agreements provide otherwise. Requests for an exception to policy are submitted in accordance with guidance contained in Department of Defense Instruction (DODI) 4500.57, *Transportation and Traffic Management,* and DOD 4515.13R, *Air Transportation Eligibility,* Chapter 10, Special Actions and Procedures.

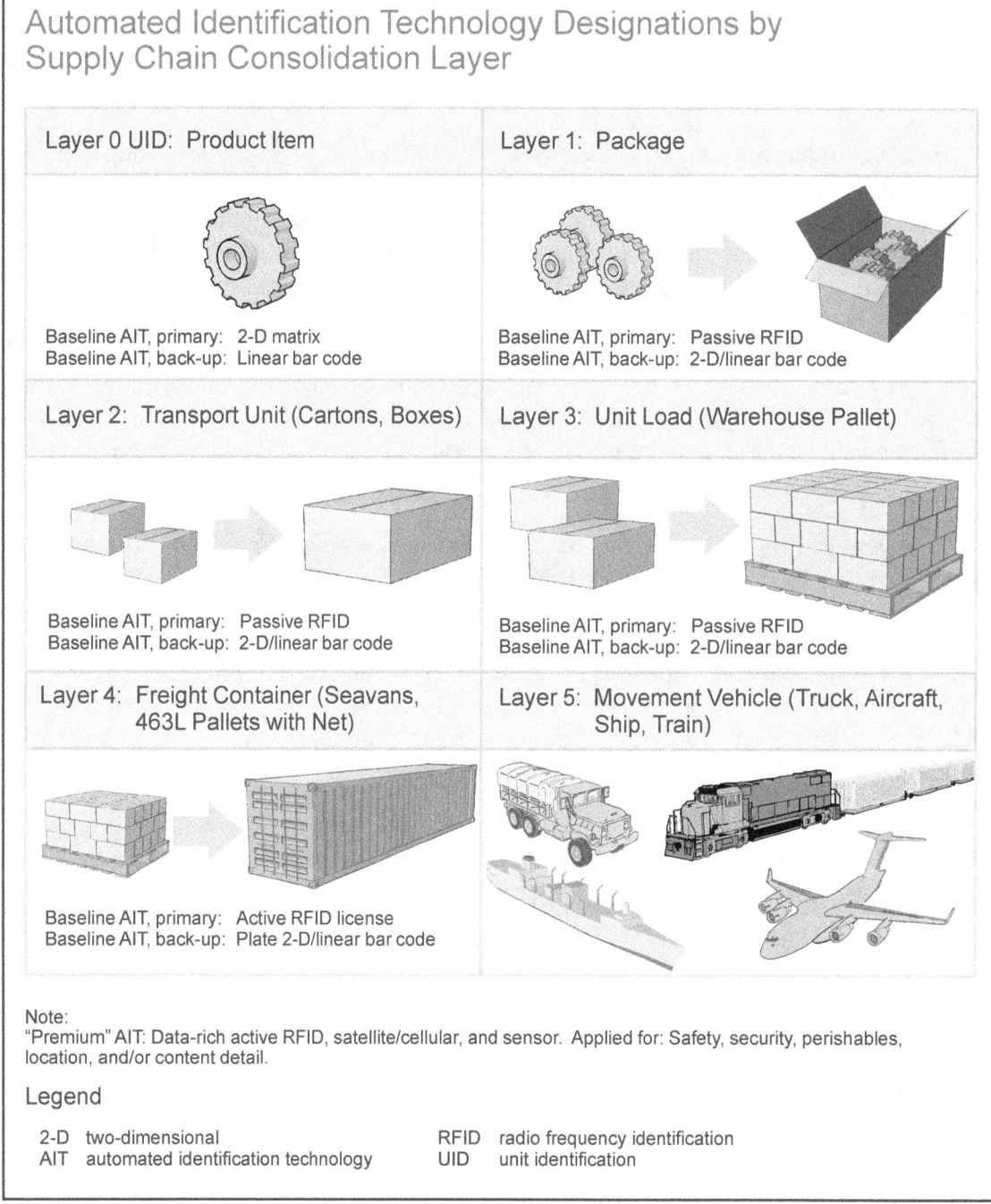

Figure IV-6. Automated Identification Technology Designations by Supply Chain Consolidation Layer

9. Customs

Background. DOD policy is to assist and cooperate with US and HN border clearance agencies in halting the flow of contraband both into the US and foreign countries. DOD enforces this policy when entry is through military channels and cooperates with other USG departments and agencies when enforcing US laws and regulations and complying with foreign requirements concerning customs, agriculture, immigration, and other border clearance requirements without unnecessarily delaying the movement of DOD personnel and material. This policy also applies to the export of goods to and through other countries. USTRANSCOM serves as the executive agent for DOD to manage the DOD Customs and Border Clearance Program (CBCP). As executive agent, USTRANSCOM in collaboration with DOD components, USG border clearance activities and foreign governments (through the supported theater commands), manages all aspects of the DOD CBCP.

Intentionally Blank

APPENDIX A
TRANSPORTATION PRIORITIES

1. General

The effective use of DOD transportation resources to move passengers and cargo requires the establishment of transportation priorities. These assigned transportation priorities enable logistic managers to determine mode and sequence of movement in meeting both peacetime and wartime requirements. This appendix addresses the transportation priorities assigned for cargo requirements generated via MILSTRIP, cargo requirements that are non-MILSTRIP requisitions, movement of space required passengers via DOD owned and controlled transportation assets, and cargo and passenger requirements that require movement via common-user airlift and sealift resources under the DOD Transportation Movement Priority System.

2. Movement Priorities—Cargo

a. **Movement Priorities for MILSTRIP Cargo.** To ensure responsiveness, priorities used in the movement system are related to both the importance of the user's mission and the relative importance of a particular item to that mission. The UMMIPS establishes the framework and assigns indicators of mission or item importance. Force/activity designators (F/ADs) and urgency of need designators (UNDs) are used respectively to describe the importance of any given item to any specific mission.

(1) **Force/Activity Designators.** F/ADs describe the relative importance of a force, unit, activity, project, or program to accomplishing DOD objectives. There are five F/AD levels, written as Roman numerals, with F/AD I being of the highest importance. Assignment of F/AD is reserved for SecDef based upon the CJCS recommendation and criteria contained in Appendix 9 of DOD 4140.1R, *DOD Supply Chain Materiel Management Regulation,* and CJCSI 4110.01D, *Joint Materiel Priorities and Allocation.* CJCS may delegate authority to assign F/ADs II through V to the heads of DOD components and USG departments and agencies.

(2) **Urgency of Need Designators.** UNDs express the need or importance of the end use item in accomplishing the mission of the requisitioner. UNDs are identified by the letters A, B, and C, with A being the highest. The requisitioner determines the urgency of need based on criteria established by DOD.

b. **Priority Designators.** The relationship between the importance of the requisitioner's mission (F/AD) and the importance of the end item to that mission (UND) results in a priority designator (PD), sometimes called a supply priority or requisition priority. PDs are expressed as one of 15 two-digit numbers from 01 to 15, with 01 being the highest. PDs provide a means of assigning relative rankings to competing demands placed on the DOD supply system. (See Figure A-1.)

Relationship Between Urgency of Need and Force Activator Designator Produces Priority Designator			
	Urgency of Need Designator		
	A	B	C
Force Activity Designator	Requisition Priority Designator		
I	01	04	11
II	02	05	12
III	03	06	13
IV	07	09	14
V	08	10	15

Figure A-1. Relationship Between Urgency of Need and Force Activity Designator Produces Priority Designator

c. **Transportation Priorities and Shipment Modes.** The PD, when related to the required delivery date, translates into a TP. TPs are numbered 1 through 4, with 1 being the highest priority. Except for unusual circumstances, the TP drives the shipment mode (see Figure A-2). Cargo assigned TP 1 or 2 is normally air eligible unless CJCS, the cognizant shipper service, or the requisitioner stipulates otherwise. Sometimes the characteristics of the cargo (e.g., size, weight, and hazards) preclude air shipment. In these cases, the cargo is diverted to surface. Priorities for retrograde materiel movements will be established based on the criticality of the item and not on the F/AD and UND combination. Retrograde shipments fall under PD 03, 06, or 13.

Transportation Priority and Movement Conversion Table			
Supply Priority Designator	Required Delivery Date	Transportation Priority	Mode of Shipment Eligibility
01-03	All	1	Air
04-08	444, 555, 777, 1	2	Air
09-15	2	3	Surface
Not applicable	None	4	Surface

Figure A-2. Transportation Priority and Movement Conversion Table

d. **Movement Priorities for Non-MILSTRIP Cargo.** Cargo also moves as non-MILSTRIP requisitions. The Services normally designate the transportation priorities for these items, as in Figure A-3.

e. **Cargo Clearance Authorities.** Service HQ assign clearance authorities to assist DOD shippers (including DLA) in management of transportation priorities for both MILSTRIP and non-MILSTRIP cargo and correct application of transportation funds that reimburse the Transportation Working Capital Fund and pay carriers.

3. Movement Priorities—Space Required Passenger Travel via Department of Defense-Owned and-Controlled Assets

Transportation priorities for space required passenger movement will be assigned by each Service. Under normal conditions, unless CJCS directs otherwise, the passenger movement precedence will be in accordance with the USTRANSCOM or respective TCC directions that implement the single passenger reservation concept. Personnel transportation priorities are summarized below.

Transportation Priorities for Non-Military Standard
Requisitioning and Issue Procedure Cargo

Transportation Priority 1
- Defense courier division material
- Registered or certified mail
- Command and casualty report pouches
- First-class personal and official mail letters
- Personal and official priority mail parcels

Transportation Priority 2
- Other official mail parcels
- Unaccompanied baggage
- All other air-eligible mail (i.e., space-available and parcel airlift)

Transportation Priority 3
- Overseas mail and intercommand mail
- Personal property
- Nonappropriated fund mail
- Material in support of non-Department of Defense agencies

Figure A-3. Transportation Priorities for Non-Military Standard Requisitioning and Issue Procedure Cargo

a. **Transportation Priority 1**

(1) Personnel with an acute emergency that requires they be moved before everyone else and not be delayed for any reason.

(2) Medical evacuees.

(3) Personnel returning to the US or its territories on emergency leave.

b. **Transportation Priority 2**

(1) Personnel who have an urgent deadline to accomplish an essential mission at the destination station.

(2) Personnel destined for units or activities who are required to be in place to meet an emergency and whose travel is more urgent than travel under priorities 3 and 4.

(3) Personnel on temporary duty.

(4) Personnel on permanent change of station orders to mobile or moving final duty assignment.

c. **Transportation Priority 3**

(1) Personnel returning to duty station from emergency leave.

(2) Inductees traveling from military entrance processing stations to reception stations and/or training centers.

(3) Personnel on permanent change of station orders to fixed or stationary final duty assignment or duty station.

(4) Personnel movement of an urgent nature in order to accomplish an essential mission.

(5) Personnel returning to duty from routine temporary duty or temporary additional duty.

d. **Transportation Priority 4**

(1) Personnel who are otherwise eligible for movement.

(2) Dependents.

(3) Personnel of non-DOD activities.

(4) Registrants traveling from home to military entrance processing stations for processing.

Travel priorities for space-available passengers are listed in DOD 4515.13R, Air Transportation Eligibility, *Chapter 6, "Space-Available Travel."*

4. Department of Defense Transportation Movement Priority System

a. An urgency of need or the existence of valid circumstances to use a priority other than normal channel lift must be established by competent authority before these priorities can be used. Specific lift priorities are defined in CJCSI 4120.02, *Assignment of Movement and Mobility Priority.*

b. When requirements for lift exceed capability, lift managers should apply capability to the highest priority category first.

c. Lift priorities are intended to support intertheater deployments into the supported GCC's AOR and do not address retrograde movements. Retrograde movements including cargo (e.g., repairable items, containers), passengers (including noncombatant evacuation operations) and patients, and their associated lift priority, are a responsibility of the supported CCDR. Scheduling of these movement requirements should be accomplished by the GCC's JMC. Every consideration should be given to synchronizing the movement of retrograde requirements on aircraft returning from the AOR to optimize available lift and preclude the requirement to send an empty aircraft to pick them up. Specific guidance and priorities are established by the supported CCDR in an operation order and/or contingency environment, consistent with the overall operations.

APPENDIX B
CHARTER OF THE CHAIRMAN OF THE JOINT CHIEFS OF STAFF JOINT TRANSPORTATION BOARD

1. Mission

The CJCS JTB may be convened by CJCS during wartime or contingencies for ensuring President and SecDef requirements for all common-user transportation resources assigned or available to DOD are apportioned and scheduled to optimize accomplishment of DOD objectives.

2. Responsibility

The CJCS JTB acts on behalf of CJCS in the performance of functions listed in paragraph five. The Chairman of the CJCS JTB has been delegated decision authority in these areas except when a matter cannot be resolved within the CJCS JTB. In such instances, the matter is referred to CJCS for decision.

3. Membership

The CJCS JTB is composed of the following:

a. **Chairman.** Vice Director for Logistics, Joint Staff J-4.

b. **Principal Members**

    (1) Vice Director for Operations, Joint Staff Operations Directorate.

    (2) CCMD(s) operations directorate of a joint staff (J-3) and/or J-4.

c. **Supporting Members**

    (1) Deputy Director for Intelligence, Directorate for Intelligence, Joint Staff.

    (2) Vice Director for Plans, Joint Staff J-5.

    (3) Vice Director for Joint Force Development, Joint Staff Joint Force Development Directorate (J-7).

    (4) USTRANSCOM Director for Operations and Plans.

    (5) Force provider J-3 and/or J-4 equivalent.

    (6) Deputy Chief of Staff, G-4.

    (7) Director, Supply Programs and Policy Division, Deputy Chief of Naval Operations (Logistics), US Navy.

(8) Director, Logistics Plans, Policies, and Strategic Mobility Division, Installation and Logistics Department, US Marine Corps.

(9) Director of Logistics Readiness, Deputy Chief of Staff, Logistics, US Air Force.

(10) Director, DLA Logistics Operations.

d. **Secretary of CJCS JTB.** Chief, Mobility Division, Joint Staff J-4.

4. Management Concept of Combined Joint Chiefs of Staff Joint Transportation Board

When convened, the CJCS JTB acts for CJCS to communicate President and SecDef priorities and adjudicate competing requirements for intertheater mobility lift assets. The CJCS JTB also resolves other issues that negatively impact DTS and which USTRANSCOM and the supported CCDR(s) are unable to resolve. USTRANSCOM allocates transportation assets to supported CCDRs' validated requirements in accordance with the CJCS apportionment guidance and priority assigned to each operation and/or requirement. USTRANSCOM advises the Joint Staff J-3 and J-4 when movement requirements exceed capabilities. CDRUSTRANSCOM will refer problems with recommended COAs to CJCS for resolution or adjudication if a balance of transportation requirements and capabilities cannot be maintained. Should additional support be required to resolve lift shortfalls, the CJCS JTB may be convened to analyze proposed solutions and develop recommended COAs for CJCS approval.

5. Functions

Once convened, the CJCS JTB performs the following:

a. Adjudicate competing lift requirements.

b. When required, evaluate COAs being proposed or taken by CDRUSTRANSCOM to resolve conflicting transportation requirements and make appropriate recommendations to CJCS.

c. Transmit CJCS guidance to CDRUSTRANSCOM and the supported CCDRs.

d. Understand the projected operational activities of the CCDRs and the strategic direction issued by the President and SecDef to anticipate developing problems or future resource requirements.

e. When needed, provide an interface among supported and supporting CCDRs, the Chiefs of the Services, other departments and agencies, and CJCS on matters concerning transportation.

6. Procedures

CJCS JTB follows the procedures below:

a. As directed by the CJCS JTB chairman, meet in open or general sessions, which may be followed by closed or executive sessions (a video-teleconference may be the most prudent and expedient method).

b. Refer to CJCS matters that cannot be resolved within the CJCS JTB.

c. Coordinate with DOD and other departments and agencies as necessary in connection with CJCS JTB duties.

d. Invite appropriate representatives from agencies involved in issues before the board to attend meetings of the CJCS JTB and/or the CJCS JTB Secretariat.

e. When appropriate, approve the requests of DOD agencies and other offices to attend meetings of the CJCS JTB and/or the CJCS JTB Secretariat.

f. Establish standing operating procedures.

7. The Combined Joint Chiefs of Staff Joint Transportation Board Secretariat

The CJCS JTB Secretariat is established as an agency of the CJCS JTB to staff issues and present background, alternatives, and decision packages to the CJCS JTB for consideration. The CJCS JTB Secretariat includes the following members and representatives:

a. **Membership**

(1) **Chairman.** Chief, Mobility Division, Joint Staff J-4.

(2) **J-3 Representative.** Chief, Joint Operations Division.

(3) **J-5 Representative.** Chief, Strategy Division/Chief, Conventional War Plans Division.

(4) **J-7 Representative.**

(5) **USTRANSCOM Representative.** USTRANSCOM Joint Staff Liaison Officer.

(6) **Force Provider.** Normally will be force provider director, J-3 or J-4 equivalent.

(7) **Army Representative.** Chief, Strategic Mobility Division Director for Force Projection and Distribution, Office of the Deputy Chief of Staff for Logistics (US Army).

(8) **Air Force Representative.** Chief, Deployment and Distribution Management, Directorate of Logistics Readiness, Deputy Chief of Staff, Installation and Logistics.

(9) **Navy Representative.** Head, Logistics Operations Programs.

(10) **Marine Corps Representative.** Head, Logistics Plans and Operations Branch, Logistics Plans, Policies, and Strategic Mobility Division.

(11) **Reserve and Guard Representative.** Assistants to the Chairman for National Guard and Reserve Matters.

(12) **DLA Representative.** DLA Joint Staff Liaison Officer.

b. **Representation.** The secretary and/or recorder, CJCS JTB Secretariat, will be provided by the Joint Staff J-4. When activated, Joint Staff members will provide information, briefing, and administrative support to the CJCS JTB Secretariat as required.

8. Functions of the Combined Joint Chiefs of Staff Joint Transportation Board Secretariat

The CJCS JTB Secretariat is responsible for the following:

a. Providing continuity for CJCS JTB.

b. Attending all meetings of CJCS JTB.

c. Preparing and publishing standing operating procedures for the conduct of the CJCS JTB and the CJCS JTB Secretariat; furnish support required.

d. Having current transportation and strategic movement requirements and capabilities data updated and available for meetings of the CJCS JTB.

e. Analyzing proposed COAs, evaluating expected results, and preparing presentations of the options for the CJCS JTB meetings.

f. Notifying USTRANSCOM and the CJCS JTB of identified or anticipated DTS problem areas while preparing for the CJCS JTB meetings.

g. Publishing the decisions of the CJCS JTB.

h. Responding to requirements of the CJCS JTB.

i. Providing a record of proceedings of each CJCS JTB and CJCS JTB Secretariat meeting.

j. Tracking the effects of the CJCS JTB actions and reporting them to the CJCS JTB director.

APPENDIX C
REFERENCES

The development of JP 4-01 is based on the following primary references:

1. General

Title 10, United States Code.

2. Department of Defense Publications

a. DOD Directive (DODD) 2010.9, *Acquisition and Cross-Servicing Agreements.*

b. DODD 4500.09E, *Transportation and Traffic Management.*

c. DODD 4510.11, *DOD Transportation Engineering.*

d. DODD 5158.04, *United States Transportation Command (USTRANSCOM).*

e. DODI 4500.17, *Proceedings Before Transportation Regulatory Bodies.*

f. DODI 4500.43, *Operational Support Airlift (OSA).*

g. DODI 4500.53, *DOD Commercial Air Transportation Quality and Safety Review Program.*

h. DODI 4500.57, *Transportation and Traffic Management.*

i. DOD Regulation 4140.1-R, *DOD Supply Chain Materiel Management Regulation.*

j. Defense Transportation Regulation (DTR) 4500.9-R, *Defense Transportation Regulation.*

k. DOD Regulation 4515.13-R, *Air Transportation Eligibility.*

3. Chairman of the Joint Chiefs of Staff Publications

a. CJCSI 2120.01, *Acquisition and Cross-Servicing Agreements.*

b. CJCSI 3110.01H, *Joint Strategic Capabilities Plan (JSCP) (U).*

c. CJCSI 3110.03D, *Logistics Supplement to the Joint Strategic Capabilities Plan (JSCP) for FY 2008.*

d. CJCSI 4110.01D, *Joint Materiel Priorities and Allocation.*

e. CJCSI 4120.01C, *Assignment of Movement and Mobility Priority.*

f. CJCSM 3122 Series, *Joint Operation Planning and Execution System.*

g. JP 1-02, *Department of Defense Dictionary of Military and Associated Terms.*

h. JP 3-17, *Air Mobility Operations.*

i. JP 3-35, *Deployment and Redeployment Operations.*

j. JP 4-0, *Joint Logistics.*

k. JP 4-01.2, *Sealift Support to Joint Operations.*

l. JP 4-01.5, *Joint Terminal Operations.*

m. JP 4-01.6, *Joint Logistics Over-the-Shore.*

n. JP 4-02, *Health Service Support.*

o. JP 4-09, *Distribution Operations.*

p. JP 6-0, *Joint Communications System.*

APPENDIX D
ADMINISTRATIVE INSTRUCTIONS

1. User Comments

Users in the field are highly encouraged to submit comments on this publication to: Joint Staff J-7, Deputy Director, Joint Education and Doctrine, ATTN: Joint Doctrine Analysis Division, 116 Lake View Parkway, Suffolk, VA 23435-2697. These comments should address content (accuracy, usefulness, consistency, and organization), writing, and appearance.

2. Authorship

The lead agent for this publication is the USTRANSCOM. The Joint Staff doctrine sponsor for this publication is the Joint Staff Director for Logistics (J-4).

3. Supersession

This publication supersedes JP 4-01, 19 March 2003, Joint Doctrine for the DTS.

4. Change Recommendations

a. Recommendations for urgent changes to this publication should be submitted:

TO: JOINT STAFF WASHINGTON DC//J7-JE&D//

b. Routine changes should be submitted electronically to the Deputy Director, Joint Education and Doctrine, ATTN: Joint Doctrine Analysis Division, 116 Lake View Parkway, Suffolk, VA 23435-2697 and info the lead agent and the Director for Joint Force Development, J-7/JE&D.

c. When a Joint Staff directorate submits a proposal to CJCS that would change source document information reflected in this publication, that directorate will include a proposed change to this publication as an enclosure to its proposal. The Services and other organizations are requested to notify the Joint Staff J-7 when changes to source documents reflected in this publication are initiated.

5. Distribution of Publications

Local reproduction is authorized and access to unclassified publications is unrestricted. However, access to and reproduction authorization for classified JPs must be in accordance with DOD Manual 5200.01, Volume 1, *DOD Information Security Program: Overview, Classification, and Declassification,* and DOD Manual 5200.01, Volume 3, *DOD Information Security Program: Protection of Classified Information.*

6. Distribution of Electronic Publications

a. Joint Staff J-7 will not print copies of JPs for distribution. Electronic versions are available on JDEIS at https://jdeis.js.mil (NIPRNET), and https://jdeis.js.smil.mil/jdeis (SIPRNET) and on the Joint Electronic Library (JEL) at http://www.dtic.mil/doctrine (NIPRNET).

b. Only approved JPs and joint test publications are releasable outside the CCMDs, Services, and Joint Staff. Release of any classified JP to foreign governments or foreign nationals must be requested through the local embassy (Defense Attaché Office) to DIA, Defense Foreign Liaison/IE-3, 200 MacDill Blvd., Joint Base Anacostia-Bolling, Washington, DC 20340-5100.

c. JEL CD-ROM. Upon request of a joint doctrine development community member, the Joint Staff J-7 will produce and deliver one CD-ROM with current JPs. This JEL CD-ROM will be updated not less than semi-annually and when received can be locally reproduced for use within the CCMDs, Services, and combat support agencies.

GLOSSARY
PART I—ABBREVIATIONS AND ACRONYMS

ACSA	acquisition and cross-servicing agreement
AIT	automated identification technology
AMC	Air Mobility Command
AMD	air mobility division
AOR	area of responsibility
APF	afloat pre-positioning force
APOD	aerial port of debarkation
APOE	aerial port of embarkation
APS	Army pre-positioned stocks
ARC	air Reserve Component
BEAR	basic expeditionary airfield resources
C2	command and control
CBCP	Customs and Border Clearance Program (DOD)
CBP	Customs and Border Protection (DHS)
CCDR	combatant commander
CCMD	combatant command
CDRUSTRANSCOM	Commander, United States Transportation Command
CHE	container-handling equipment
CIO	chief information officer
CJCS	Chairman of the Joint Chiefs of Staff
CJCSI	Chairman of the Joint Chiefs of Staff instruction
CJCSM	Chairman of the Joint Chiefs of Staff manual
CMOS	Cargo Movement Operations System (USAF)
COA	course of action
COCOM	combatant command (command authority)
CONOPS	concept of operations
CONUS	continental United States
CORE	contingency response program
CRAF	Civil Reserve Air Fleet
CULT	common-user land transportation
DDOC	Deployment and Distribution Operations Center (USTRANSCOM)
DFRIF	Defense Freight Railway Interchange Fleet
DHHS	Department of Health and Human Services
DIA	Defense Intelligence Agency
DISA	Defense Information Systems Agency
DLA	Defense Logistics Agency
DLMS	Department Logistics Management System
DOD	Department of Defense
DODD	Department of Defense directive

DODI	Department of Defense instruction
DOE	Department of Energy
DOI	Department of the Interior
DOS	Department of State
DOT	Department of Transportation
DOTEO	Department of Transportation emergency organization
DPO	distribution process owner
DTCI	Defense Transportation Coordination Initiative
DTR	Defense Transportation Regulation
DTS	Defense Transportation System
EDI	electronic data interchange
ETO	Emergency Transportation Operations (DOT)
EUSCS	effective United States-controlled ships
FAA	Federal Aviation Administration (DOT)
F/AD	force/activity designator
FEMA	Federal Emergency Management Agency (DHS)
FHA	foreign humanitarian assistance
FHWA	Federal Highway Administration (DOT)
FRA	Federal Railroad Administration (DOT)
FSS	fast sealift ship
GATES	Global Air Transportation Execution System
GCC	geographic combatant commander
GCCS	Global Command and Control System
GDSS	Global Decision Support System
GEF	Guidance for Employment of the Force
GSA	General Services Administration
GTM	global transportation management
HN	host nation
HNS	host-nation support
HQ	headquarters
IGC	Integrated Data Environment/Global Transportation Network Convergence
ITV	in-transit visibility
J-3	operations directorate of a joint staff
J-4	logistics directorate of a joint staff
J-5	plans directorate of a joint staff
J-7	operational plans and interoperability directorate of a joint staff
JDDOC	joint deployment and distribution operations center
JFC	joint force commander

JLOC	joint logistics operations center
JLOTS	joint logistics over-the-shore
JMC	joint movement center
JOPES	Joint Operation Planning and Execution System
JP	joint publication
JPAG	Joint Planning Advisory Group
JPEC	joint planning and execution community
JRSOI	joint reception, staging, onward movement, and integration
JSCP	Joint Strategic Capabilities Plan
JTB	Joint Transportation Board
JTF-PO	joint task force–port opening
JTMS	joint training master schedule
LMSR	large, medium-speed roll-on/roll-off
MAGTF	Marine air-ground task force
MARAD	Maritime Administration
MARAD RRF	Maritime Administration Ready Reserve Force
MHE	materials handling equipment
MILSTRIP	military standard requisitioning and issue procedure
MPF	maritime pre-positioning force
MPS	maritime pre-positioning ship
MSC	Military Sealift Command
MSP	maritime security program
MTF	medical treatment facility
NATO	North Atlantic Treaty Organization
NDRF	National Defense Reserve Fleet
NOAA	National Oceanic and Atmospheric Administration
NSE	Navy support element
NURP	non-unit-related personnel
OCONUS	outside the continental United States
OFDA	Office of United States Foreign Disaster Assistance (USAID)
OPCON	operational control
OPDS	offshore petroleum discharge system
OPLAN	operation plan
OPROJ	operational project
OSA	operational support airlift
PD	priority designator
PM	patient movement
POC	point of contact
POD	port of debarkation

POE	port of embarkation
POL	petroleum, oils, and lubricants
PREPO	pre-positioned force, equipment, or supplies
RFID	radio frequency identification
RO/RO	roll-on/roll-off
ROS	reduced operating status
SAAM	special assignment airlift mission
SDDC	Surface Deployment and Distribution Command
SDDCTEA	Surface Deployment and Distribution Command Transportation Engineering Agency
SecDef	Secretary of Defense
SECTRANS	Secretary of Transportation
618 AOC (TACC)	618 Air Operations Center (Tanker Airlift Control Center)
SPM	single port manager
SPOD	seaport of debarkation
SPOE	seaport of embarkation
TCC	transportation component command
TCN	transportation control number
TDP	theater distribution plan
T-JTB	theater-joint transportation board
TP	transportation priority
TPFDD	time-phased force and deployment data
TSA	Transportation Security Administration (DHS)
TTN	transportation tracking number
UCP	Unified Command Plan
UMMIPS	Uniform Material Movement and Issue Priority System
UND	urgency of need designator
USC	United States Code
USCG	United States Coast Guard
USG	United States Government
USML	United States Munitions List
USPS	United States Postal Service
USTRANSCOM	United States Transportation Command
VISA	Voluntary Intermodal Sealift Agreement
VTA	voluntary tanker agreement
WRSA	war reserve stocks for allies
WWX	worldwide express

civil transportation. The movement of persons, property, or mail by civil facilities, and the resources necessary to accomplish the movement. (Upon approval of this revised publication, this definition will modify the existing definition and be incorporated into JP 1-02.)

container. An article of transport equipment that meets American National Standards Institute/International Organization for Standardization standards that is designed to facilitate and optimize the carriage of goods by one or more modes of transportation without intermediate handling of the contents. (Upon approval of this revised publication, this definition will modify the existing definition and be incorporated into JP 1-02.)

containerization. None. (Upon approval of this revised publication, this term and its definition will be removed from JP 1-02.)

contingency response program. Fast reaction transportation procedures intended to provide for priority use of land transportation assets by Department of Defense when required. Also called **CORE.** (JP 1-02. SOURCE: JP 4-01)

Defense Transportation System. That portion of the worldwide transportation infrastructure that supports Department of Defense transportation needs in peace and war. Also called **DTS.** (Upon approval of this publication, this definition will modify the existing definition and be incorporated into JP 1-02.)

eligible traffic. None. (Upon approval of this revised publication, this term and its definition will be removed from JP 1-02.)

global transportation management. The integrated process of satisfying transportation requirements using the Defense Transportation System to meet national security objectives. Also called **GTM.** (Upon approval of this revised publication, this definition will modify the existing definition and be incorporated into JP 1-02.)

Global Transportation Network. None. (Upon approval of this revised publication, this term and its definition will be removed from JP 1-02.)

intermodal systems. None. (Upon approval of this revised publication, this term and its definition will be removed from JP 1-02.)

intertheater traffic. None. (Upon approval of this revised publication, this term and its definition will be removed from JP 1-02.)

Joint Logistics Operations Center. The Joint Logistics Operations Center is the current operations division within the Logistics Directorate of the Joint Staff, which monitors crises, exercises, and interagency actions and works acquisition and cross-servicing agreements as well as international logistics. Also called **JLOC.** (Upon approval of this revised publication, this definition will modify the existing definition and be incorporated into JP 1-02.)

Joint Transportation Board. Responsible to the Chairman of Joint Chiefs of Staff, the Joint Transportation Board assures that common-user transportation resources assigned or available to the Department of Defense are allocated to achieve maximum benefit in meeting Department of Defense objectives. Also called **JTB.** (Upon approval of this revised publication, this definition will modify the existing definition and be incorporated into JP 1-02.)

military standard requisitioning and issue procedure. A uniform procedure established by the Department of Defense for use within the Department of Defense to govern requisition and issue of materiel within standardized priorities. Also called **MILSTRIP.** (Upon approval of this revised publication, this publication will assume proponency for this term and its definition and this publication number will be added to JP 1-02.)

priority designator. A two-digit issue and priority code placed in military standard requisitioning and issue procedure requisitions to provide a means of assigning relative rankings to competing demands placed on the Department of Defense supply system. (Upon approval of this revised publication, this definition will modify the existing definition and be incorporated into JP 1-02.)

Service-organic transportation assets. Transportation assets that are assigned to a Military Department for functions of the Secretaries of the Military Departments set forth in Title 10, United States Code, Sections 3013(b), 5013(b), and 8013(b). (Upon approval of this revised publication, this definition will modify the existing definition and be incorporated into JP 1-02.)

single manager. A Military Department or agency designated by the Secretary of Defense to be responsible for management of specified commodities or common service activities on a Department of Defense-wide basis. (Upon approval of this revised publication, this definition will modify the existing definition and be incorporated into JP 1-02.)

single manager for transportation. The United States Transportation Command is the Department of Defense single manager for transportation, other than Service-organic or theater-assigned transportation assets. (JP 1-02. SOURCE: JP 4-01)

space assignment. An assignment to the individual Military Departments/Services by the appropriate transportation operating agency of movement capability which completely or partially satisfies the stated requirements of the Military Departments/Services for the operating month and that has been accepted by them without the necessity for referral to the Joint Transportation Board for allocation. (Upon approval of this revised publication, this definition will modify the existing definition and be incorporated into JP 1-02.)

special assignment airlift requirements. None. (Upon approval of this revised publication, this term and its definition will be removed from JP 1-02.)

strategic mobility. The capability to deploy and sustain military forces worldwide in support of national strategy. (Upon approval of this revised publication, this term and its definition will be included in JP 1-02.)

theater-assigned transportation assets. Transportation assets that are assigned under the CCMD (command authority) of a geographic combatant commander. (JP 1-02. SOURCE: JP 4-01)

theater distribution system. A distribution system comprised of four independent and mutually supported networks within theater to meet the geographic combatant commander's requirements: the physical network; the financial network; the information network; and the communications network. (JP 1-02. SOURCE: JP 4-01).

transportability. None. (Upon approval of this revised publication, this term and its definition will be removed from JP 1-02.)

transportation emergency. None. (Upon approval of this revised publication, this term and its definition will be removed from JP 1-02.)

transportation movement requirement. None. (Upon approval of this revised publication, this term and its definition will be removed from JP 1-02.)

transportation system. All the land, water, and air routes and transportation assets engaged in the movement of United States forces and their supplies during military operations, involving both mature and immature theaters and at the strategic, operational, and tactical levels of war. (Upon approval of this revised publication, this publication will assume proponency for this term and this definition will modify the existing definition and be incorporated into JP 1-02.)

United States Transportation Command. None. (Upon approval of this revised publication, this term and its definition will be removed from JP 1-02.)

Worldwide Port System. None. (Upon approval of this revised publication, this term and its definition will be removed from JP 1-02.)

Intentionally Blank

JOINT DOCTRINE PUBLICATIONS HIERARCHY

JP 1
JOINT DOCTRINE
JP 1-0
PERSONNEL
JP 2-0
INTELLIGENCE
JP 3-0
OPERATIONS
JP 4-0
LOGISTICS
JP 5-0
PLANS
JP 6-0
COMMUNICATIONS SYSTEM

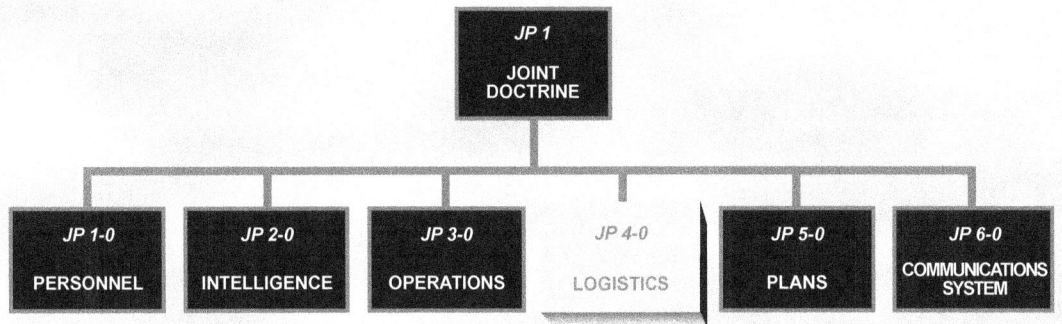

All joint publications are organized into a comprehensive hierarchy as shown in the chart above. **Joint Publication (JP) 4-01** is in the **Logistics** series of joint doctrine publications. The diagram below illustrates an overview of the development process:

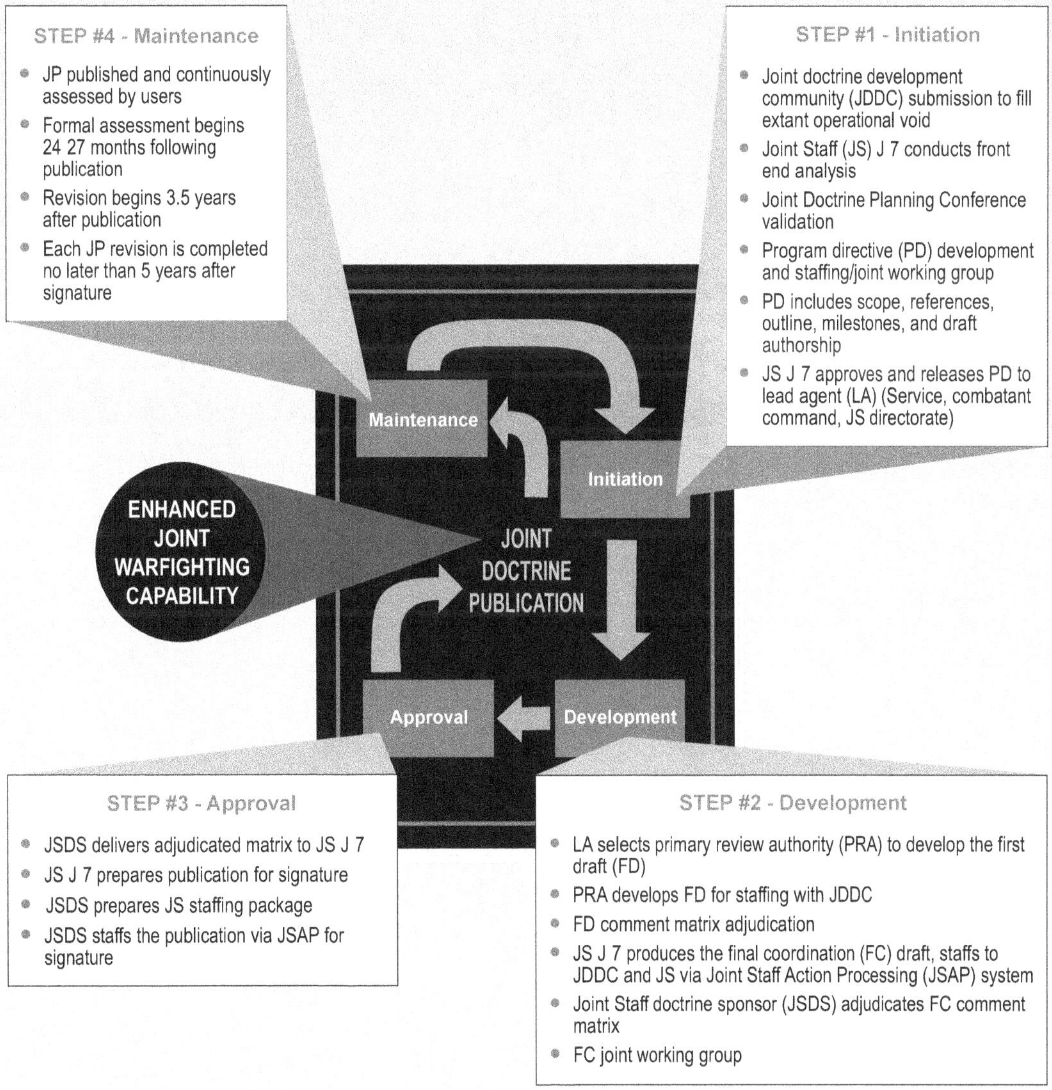

STEP #4 - Maintenance
JP published and continuously assessed by users
Formal assessment begins 24 27 months following publication
Revision begins 3.5 years after publication
Each JP revision is completed no later than 5 years after signature
STEP #1 - Initiation
Joint doctrine development community (JDDC) submission to fill extant operational void
Joint Staff (JS) J 7 conducts front end analysis
Joint Doctrine Planning Conference validation
Program directive (PD) development and staffing/joint working group
PD includes scope, references, outline, milestones, and draft authorship
JS J 7 approves and releases PD to lead agent (LA) (Service, combatant command, JS directorate)
Maintenance
Initiation
ENHANCED JOINT WARFIGHTING CAPABILITY
JOINT DOCTRINE PUBLICATION
Approval
Development
STEP #3 - Approval
JSDS delivers adjudicated matrix to JS J 7
JS J 7 prepares publication for signature
JSDS prepares JS staffing package
JSDS staffs the publication via JSAP for signature
STEP #2 - Development
LA selects primary review authority (PRA) to develop the first draft (FD)
PRA develops FD for staffing with JDDC
FD comment matrix adjudication
JS J 7 produces the final coordination (FC) draft, staffs to JDDC and JS via Joint Staff Action Processing (JSAP) system
Joint Staff doctrine sponsor (JSDS) adjudicates FC comment matrix
FC joint working group

www.ingramcontent.com/pod-product-compliance
Lightning Source LLC
Chambersburg PA
CBHW081328310526
45789CB00018B/2550